Cambridge Elements ≡

Elements in Contentious Politics
edited by
David S. Meyer
University of California, Irvine
Suzanne Staggenborg
University of Pittsburgh

SIXTY YEARS OF VISIBLE PROTEST IN THE DISABILITY STRUGGLE FOR EQUALITY, JUSTICE, AND INCLUSION

David Pettinicchio
University of Toronto

CAMBRIDGE
UNIVERSITY PRESS

Shaftesbury Road, Cambridge CB2 8EA, United Kingdom

One Liberty Plaza, 20th Floor, New York, NY 10006, USA

477 Williamstown Road, Port Melbourne, VIC 3207, Australia

314–321, 3rd Floor, Plot 3, Splendor Forum, Jasola District Centre,
New Delhi – 110025, India

103 Penang Road, #05–06/07, Visioncrest Commercial, Singapore 238467

Cambridge University Press is part of Cambridge University Press & Assessment,
a department of the University of Cambridge.

We share the University's mission to contribute to society through the pursuit of
education, learning and research at the highest international levels of excellence.

www.cambridge.org
Information on this title: www.cambridge.org/9781009497923

DOI: 10.1017/9781009497893

First published 2024

A catalogue record for this publication is available from the British Library.

ISBN 978-1-009-49792-3 Hardback
ISBN 978-1-009-49788-6 Paperback
ISSN 2633-3570 (online)
ISSN 2633-3562 (print)

Sixty Years of Visible Protest in the Disability Struggle for Equality, Justice, and Inclusion

Elements in Contentious Politics

DOI: 10.1017/9781009497893
First published online: March 2024

David Pettinicchio
University of Toronto

Author for correspondence: David Pettinicchio, d.pettinicchio@utoronto.ca

Abstract: Visible protests reflect both continuity and change. This Element illustrates how protest around long-standing issues and grievances is punctuated by movement dynamics as well as broader cultural and institutional environments. The disability movement is an example of how activist networks and groups strategically adapt to opportunity and threat, linking protest waves to the development of issue politics. The Element examines sixty years of protest across numerous issue areas that matter for disability including social welfare, discrimination, transportation, healthcare, and media portrayals. Situating visible protest in this way provides a more nuanced picture of cycles of contention as they relate to political and organizational processes, strategies and tactics, and short-and-long-term outcomes. It also provides clues about why protest ebbs and flows, when and how protest matters, who it matters for, and for what.

This Element also has a video abstract: www.cambridge.org/Pettinicchio

Keywords: social movements, social change, protest outcomes, disruption, disability rights

ISBNs: 9781009497923 (HB), 9781009497886 (PB), 9781009497893 (OC)
ISSNs: 2633-3570 (online), 2633-3562 (print)

Contents

1 Mobilizing against Inequality

In 2019, disability activist Jennifer Bartlett joined the New York Metropolitan Transit Authority (MTA) President's Office for Systemwide Accessibility. Before that, she led the Elevator Action Group. Its main target was the MTA seeking to ensure that accessibility remain a top policy priority. It is one of several "action groups" within Rise and Resist (RAR), an organization formed in response to emerging threats associated with Donald Trump and the 2016 US presidential election. That year, Bartlett organized a protest purposely coinciding with the Women's March. The event's links to a broader network of New York based activists as well as the Women's March raised visibility and helped expose inaccessible transit to a wide audience receiving considerable media coverage. In addition to getting a place at the table, Bartlett's protest achieved its main objective: broadcasting grievances and goals to new activists and conscience constituents (Della Porta and Mattoni 2014). This case demonstrates how threats turned into opportunities for new groups and activists to energize public discourse on long-standing grievances like inaccessibility.

Bartlett and the Elevator Action Group also found new opportunities to challenge the very movements aligned with their cause. The Women's Marches were not accessible to all activists. As a RAR newsletter noted, "The Disabled Women's Non-March is a response to the Women's March Alliance's failure to fully engage around disability justice and accessibility, and a celebration of the contributions that disabled women make to the resistance movement and to the world at large."[1] Activists saw the protest as a success. Not only did it increase visibility of a core movement grievance (inaccessible public transit), it drew attention to a system and culture of disabling environments inside and outside of the movement.

Accessible transportation dates back to the origins of the disability movement in the early 1970s. It is an issue area that subsequently helped define a second visible protest wave in the 1980s and 1990s, generating some of the most disruptive protests in the movement's sixty-year history. Rise and Resist helped to recenter inaccessibility around the social justice issues of the Women's March in the third disability protest wave creating a path for disability activists to address exclusion within the broader American Resistance movement.

These recent examples of disability movement mobilization raise several key questions I seek to answer in this work: Why do protest waves (re)emerge when they do in addressing long-time grievances? How do factors like political opportunities, threats, and organizational resources mobilize discontent? What do protest waves say about the relationship between elites and challengers over

---

[1] riseandresist.medium.com.

time and across the different issue areas movements work in? How do grievances, political processes, and groups and networks maintain continuity
between waves and what does this mean for elite-challenger interactions,
targets, strategies, and tactics? What are the outcomes of visible protest in
challenging inequalities?

Bartlett, RAR, and the Elevator Action Group's efforts reflect elements of
change and continuity. They were part of the American Resistance – an historical moment which reframed long-standing inequalities evermore so around
entrenched systemic oppression and structural injustice, providing new opportunities, tools, and resources for disability activists. It helped tie the disability
cause to various other cause fields including racial justice, the women's movement, immigration rights, reproductive rights, and the LGBTQ movement. By
situating disability alongside and as intersecting with other marginalized statuses, contemporary mobilizing efforts placed front and center the relational and
contextual dimensions of inequality illustrating how inequality, exploitation,
exclusion, and injustice are grievances shared by multiple communities and
constituencies (Maroto and Pettinicchio 2022; Tomaskovic-Devey and Avent-
Holt 2019).

Activists also thought their protests were having an impact. Disability activists in the Resistance took credit for preventing the repeal of the Affordable Care
Act along with other social welfare policies. They managed to put pressure on
the Democratic Party to take its grassroots elements more seriously, distinguish-
ing the Resistance from prior large-scale coalitions (Fisher and Nasrin 2021)
like those mobilized in the Reagan era (Pettinicchio 2019). Their efforts were
a reminder that disability remains a chief axis of inequality in contemporary
society (Mauldin and Brown 2021).

At the same time, many of the underlying factors recently mobilizing disability activists were variations of the same grievances that mobilized activists in
the first and second waves tied to the same key issue areas like social welfare,
health, and transportation. The collective efforts of numerous communities
brought together by the Resistance punctuated a third wave of disability activism that began in the late 2000s following the decline of the second protest wave
and a relative period of quiescence or abeyance (Rupp and Taylor 1987). Transit
protests have ebbed and flowed over the last sixty years, seeing successes, as
well as continued challenges. The same is true for another core disability
movement issue: the fight for home or community-based care. It is an area
that has also seen progress, as well as pushback, rollbacks, and threat, which
continue to mobilize activists.

Although grievances have often been discounted in favor of political process
models and the role of organizational resources in shaping mobilization,

grievances do tell us something about what has changed, but also what remains unresolved. It is difficult to link the emergence and decline of protest waves to grievances which are seemingly constant. Yet, grievances remain relevant for understanding protest when activists and groups meaningfully convert grievances into movement objectives, situate them in relation to the goals of protest, and challenge relevant targets of action. These efforts then point to other endogenous factors (i.e., organizations, networks) and exogenous factors (opportunities, threats) that explain the structure and timing of protest (Opp 1988). Protest waves reflect new opportunities for movements to activate preexisting grievances where threats and backtracking *regularly* play a role.

1.1 The Regularity of Protest

Much has been written about why movement activity seems to come and go. Tarrow's (1994) classic cycles of contention identifies a regularity in protest – that protest activity rises, intensifies, and subsides, only to resurface once again. This suggests that issue areas experience periodic instability (Baumgartner and Jones 1993) potentially because they remain open or unsettled even after intense periods of grassroots and elite activity. This also implies that grievances are not totally resolved, or that partial gains lead to future discontent fueling subsequent mobilization. Extant grievances may be activated by new exogenous developments including threats – like the rise of Trump – which refocuses movement resources on orchestrating visible disruptive action. Accordingly, social movement scholars rightfully highlight the interplay between political opportunity, threat, and resources motivating visible protest wave (re)emergence (Koopmans 2004).

Tactics like visible protest became a routine part of the disability movement's repertoire because early in the first wave, disruptive attention-grabbing protests were generally seen by activists and the media as achieving some success (Soule 1999) – whether success involved getting material change like policy reform or meetings with elites, or raising broad awareness of inequality. Early in the first disability protest wave, a nationwide seventeen-day sit-in targeted regional offices of the Health, Education, and Welfare Department in April 1977 for failing to sign Section 504 regulations – the rights and antidiscrimination language in the 1973 Rehabilitation Act. Even though disability activists and groups had been working with elites to expand disability rights, when it came to implementation, activists increasingly saw institutional activism and the use of regular political channels as unable to effect change on its own (Pettinicchio 2012).

Protesters including movement leader and founder of the group Disabled in Action (DIA), Judy Heumann, held vigils day and night, met with some administration officials and allies in Congress, writing letters demanding that regulations be signed. Disabled in Action was joined by the newly created American Coalition of Citizens with Disabilities (ACCD) and more established groups like Paralyzed Veterans of America (PVA) and the National Paraplegia Foundation both founded in 1946. Signing the regulations was seen as a movement success – materially and symbolically – providing activists with a sense of collective efficacy that visible protests directly helped to produce positive change, at least for the time being.

Waves reflect distinct historical moments within which strategic innovations like visible protests are organized, implemented, and then presumably, lead to some outcome. As Maher et al. (2019) claim, "understanding movement protest activity depends on the particular historical moment of interest," such that opportunities, resources, and frames are a function of both externalities and internal movement dynamics in each period. Protest waves also embody adaptation to new realities (Tilly 1978). Adaptation might mean borrowing and tweaking tactics from prior waves, borrowing from efforts in one issue area and applying it to another, and from other social movements altogether. For example, in the first disability protest wave, stopping traffic to protest inequalities in public transit, sit-ins and ride-ins, and creating human blockades, were tactics borrowed from the Black civil rights and women's movements. These became part of the disability movement's tactical repertoire across all its protest waves. Not only that, but the expansion of minority rights to other constituencies (Skrentny 2002) and the rise of institutionalized and professional advocacy (Minkoff 1999) in the 1970s shaped the internal dynamics of the disability movement making protests more viable.

This had important consequences for the second and third disability visible protest waves. As relatively short-term events, visible protests were transformative for the disability rights movement, producing longer-term impacts not just for subsequent protests, but for the structure and culture of the movement more generally (Della Porta 2011; Sewell 2005; Wood et al. 2017). Visible protests set the tone for the ongoing interactions between activists and elites often over a similar core set of grievances. The interaction between challengers and elites is marked by a series of social movement outcomes. Each protest failure, success, or more likely something in between, shaped what was next for activists.

Protest waves bring to light the ways in which movements adapt to new organizational and resource environments as well changing issue politics which may be peppered by both new opportunities and threats. These include the passage and implementation of the Rehabilitation Act in the mid-1970s, Reagan and the rights counterrevolution of the 1980s, the alleged failures of the Americans with Disabilities Act in the 1990s, the fight against so-called unfunded mandates in the 1990s, the rise of Trump and the Resistance in 2016, and so on. The realities of these political developments reflect their own dynamics, but they, like mobilization, also reflect the political and movement processes that led up to those moments.

Issues and movements are intertwined and move together influencing each other in non-recursive ways. Perhaps not surprisingly, the way opportunities and threats across historical moments motivated direct action shared a lot in common. Social Movement Organizations (SMOs) and activists adapt tactics and strategies based on what groups and actors believed worked in similar past circumstances. These mobilizing structures too are an important dimension of continuity. Protest waves carry with them the experiences and developments that came with prior waves sustained by activists and groups via so-called submerged networks (Melucci 1996) even when protest activity appears to wane or move into periods of abeyance. These continuities are fostered by collective memory, organizational and tactical experience, and ongoing interactions between challengers and targets that do not simply disappear, but rather adapt to new circumstances. Adaptation may mean shifting efforts away from visible protest, to less attention-drawing tactics like lobbying, lawsuits, and regular meetings with elites.

1.2 Protest within and between Issue Areas

The disability movement is not a single-issue movement. As I have already alluded to, core disability movement grievances are embedded in defined issue areas: employment, transportation, healthcare, education, social welfare, rights and discrimination, and media depictions of disability. This also means that each is governed by its own issue politics informing issue-specific political opportunities, threats, tactics, goals, and outcomes.

Opportunities and resources may activate grievances closely tied to a specific issue area, like for example, discrimination in the 1970s. Opportunities and resources may be largely absent in other areas within the same period, like media representations. It therefore makes sense that some issue areas experience more activity than others across each visible protest wave. With each subsequent wave, discrimination protests declined significantly while protests around media representations increased significantly.

The rise and fall of protest waves depends in large part on how politics and social movements interact with multiple issue areas simultaneously. But issue areas are not impermeable silos and core grievances around inequality and injustice transcend these issue boundaries. Healthcare and rights/discrimination are a good example of how developments in one issue area like disability antidiscrimination impacted the way policymakers and activists understood Medicaid, Social Security, and the provision of nursing home and home-based care. The same can be said for transportation. Transportation moved from a service-provision problem, to one of civil rights because of the work of activists and elites.

Additionally, threats and opportunities coupled with movement responses in one issue area can shape issue politics and mobilization in another. New opportunities around public transit accessibility which drew from the politics of rights mobilized activists and groups and, when threats of backtracking surfaced, protest groups like Americans Disabled for Accessible Public Transit (ADAPT) helped sustain protest in the area of public transit. When later, in the second protest wave, new political opportunities around healthcare reform surfaced, ADAPT (now called Americans Disabled for *Attendant Programs Today*) diverted its protest efforts to home care, given the perceived success of its transit-related protests.

Mobilization across issue areas is therefore also connected through the SMOs orchestrating visible protests. More formal disability organizations were emerging out of activist networks throughout the first protest wave in the 1970s promoting and sustaining the use of visible disruptive protest (see Figure 1). Groups like DIA, ACCD, and later ADAPT heavily associated with the use of early disruptive protests, were by disabled people for disabled people. Their memberships soon cut across disability type. And, although many nascent groups were motivated by problems tied to specific issues like public transit, antidiscrimination laws, or social welfare, they began linking grievances and

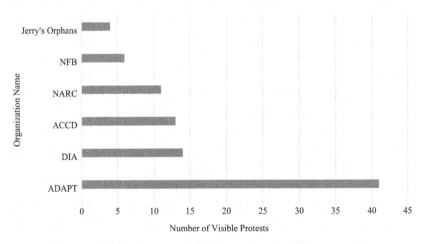

Figure 1 Disability organizations most associated with visible protests, 1961–2021

mobilizing efforts to broader inequalities that cut across issues. This represented a major change in the disability organizational field (Pettinicchio 2019).

Focusing on issue areas is more conducive to linking together protest activity, protest goals, and protest outcomes. Roughly about half the time, disability protest events experience failure and about a quarter of the time, protest waves end up constituting a series of partial victories. Outcomes vary across issue areas where outcomes may not lead to resolutions further down the road, even if objectives are met with success in the short term. Both homecare and accessible public transit are salient examples of wave after wave of successes and failures that kept grievances on the table. More recently, these issues were re-energized in a context of new political, social, and cultural norms which included the efforts of BLM, #MeToo, the Women's Marches, and the Resistance. Disability activists saw new opportunities to tie their outstanding issues of accessibility and the right to homecare to a fight about broader structural inequalities challenging a privileged, ableist, heteronormative, White status quo.

But even Resistors modeled their activism on the decades-old activism of the civil rights and disability rights movements which mobilized around a not too-different-set of grievances like inaccessible spaces, poverty and economic pre-carity, discrimination, and barriers to adequate healthcare. Indeed, on the 2019 Non-March Facebook page, a statement reads, "the disability justice movement goes far beyond access ... As the social model of disability details, we may be impaired by our bodies or mind, but it is the daily prejudice we face, as well as inaccessible spaces, that disable us." Overhead, a photograph of a 1970s protest organized by disability rights leader and founder of DIA, Judy Heumann.

1.3 The Three Waves of Visible Disability Protest

The first disability protest wave is intimately connected to important policy developments beginning in the late 1960s including efforts to make transit and public buildings accessible. This eventually led to more forceful rights legisla-tion like Section 504 of the Rehabilitation Act and the Education for All Handicapped Children Act. By the mid-1970s, disability activists had new policy tools at their disposal that helped transform disability politics, if not social policy more broadly in the US (Pettinicchio 2012, 2019; Scotch 2001). But the first wave also includes "reactive mobilization" (Van Dyke and Soule 2002) where visible protests were responding to threats and prospective losses that do much to mobilize constituents perhaps even more so than the prospect of new gains (Almeida 2019; Snow et al. 1998). Just as critical legislative gains were made, Nixon vetoed the Rehabilitation Act twice, the administration showed reluctance in enforcing rights laws, the Supreme Court went even

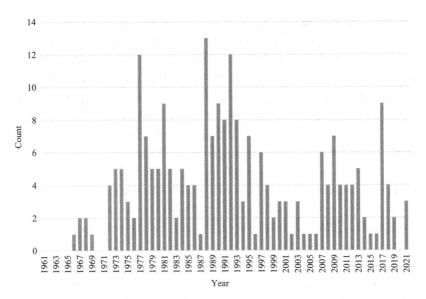

Figure 2 Disability visible protests, 1961–2022, *n* = 234

further to narrow the scope of disability rights laws (notably in *Davis v. Southeastern Community College*), and by the end of the 1970s, opposition to disability social policy seemed to be coming from all sectors. Thus, both the availability of new policy and organizational resources and threat by way of policy retrenchment went a long way in sustaining the first protest wave (see Figure 2).

These early disability visible protests had a long-term impact on the disability movement. They were seen as useful and successful in addressing grievances very early in the disability rights struggle. On November 3, 1972, about thirty disability activists blocked traffic in Manhattan followed by a second staging of fourteen protesters later that day on Madison Avenue.[2] Protesters had two objectives: to get Nixon and his reelection campaign to publicly speak about his veto and second, to get "the public to be aware of the plight of the handicapped." This and the protests to come would certainly do that. They were a model for the transit protests that soon followed and served as a model for protest in subsequent waves.

Early movement leaders challenging entrenched norms and attitudes about disability like Ed Roberts, Judy Heumann, Eunice Fiorito, and Julius Shaw were joined by growing networks of activists in San Francisco and New York City. By the early 1970s, new organizational resources became available to activists.

---

[2] Disabled Tie Up Traffic Here to Protest Nixon Aid-Bill Vote, *New York Times*, November 3, 1972.

Heumann sought to build stronger ties among people with disabilities[3] high-lighting their common struggles as opposed to their individual differences. In an interview published on DIA's webpage,[4] Heumann remembers her role in helping to create the modern disability rights movement:

> I think DIA was a very important organization at the time because it was cross disability, it did deal with multiple issues, it was a political activist organiza-tion, made no bones about it, wasn't shy about it. Really felt that we had to take what we considered the anger and oppression that we were experiencing as disabled people and not sit around and complain about it. But basically really create an agenda for change and to work collaboratively with other people and other organizations. I think that was a very strong premise of the organization but we really felt that we wanted to be thoughtful and thorough in any of the work that we were doing but we didn't want to be daunted.

Heumann saw opportunities to build a political constituency by activating existing grievances around numerous key issues and energize activists in a productive way to effect change. Both inaccessible transit and the lack of disability rights regula-tions following the passage of the Rehabilitation Act fueled much of the early part of the first wave of protest. In December 1976, activists in the newly founded ACCD led by Eunice Fiorino protested the opening of an inaccessible DC transit station – Gallery Place. The General Services Administration waved a prior court ruling that prevented the inaccessible station from opening under the 1968 Architectural Barriers Act. One of the protesters told reporters that the decision to open the station means he was "reclassified not as a second-class citizen because I'm Black, but third-class because I'm a disabled individual."[5] Protest worked, and Metro promised the station would be accessible in one year.[6] The late-70s saw other successful transit protests by ACCD. By 1981, the American Public Transportation Association (APTA) estimated that about 30 percent of all public

---

[3] In my writing, I refer to both "people with disabilities" and "disabled people" to follow how different people with disabilities refer to themselves. Although person-first language has become more common within the social sciences and among researchers, many individuals within the disability community prefer to use identity-first language because it better demonstrates how disability is a political identity.

[4] www.disabledinaction.org/heumann.html.

[5] Gallery Pl. Station Opens to Protest, *Washington Post*, December 16, 1976

[6] In addition to public transit, in 1978, blind protesters, many associated with the long-time advocacy group National Federation of the Blind (NFB) chanted "Fly me cane and all" targeting FAA regulations requiring canes be stowed (meaning blind passengers would not have access to them during the flight). Activists had been in talks for possible compromise over folding canes and lawyers filed suit in DC as well. In addition to visible protest, blind passengers were victorious in a 1978 court case (Blind Picket to Keep Canes on Planes, *Los Angeles Times*, July 6, 1978). Still, regulations today are unclear about airlines asking or requiring blind passengers to stow or give up their canes. Airlines continue to receive thousands of complaints from blind passengers (https://nfb.org/sites/default/files/images/nfb/publications/bm/bm18/bm1809/bm180908.htm).

transit buses now had lifts and although this was nowhere near the goal of total accessibility, it is important to note that just a few years earlier, there were no accessible buses.[7] It is a good example of the kinds of partial success associated with protest, the ongoing resistance against fully addressing grievances, and the tentative nature of conflict resolution.

By the end of the 1970s, the disability rights movement found itself up against growing efforts to slide back on rights across numerous issue areas including education, social welfare, and health. In August 1979, the ACCD held a demonstration at the West LA Federal Building protesting the Davis decision, joined by Ed Roberts and the AFL-CIO. Protesters held banners reading "U.S. Supreme Court handicaps the disabled" and "Congress giveth ... The Supreme Court taketh away July 11, 1979." Roberts felt betrayed. He told reporters "The Carter Administration made tremendous commitments ... Not only have they not delivered but they actually have hindered us and made it very difficult to get new legislation to help us take our place in the mainstream."[8] For activists, Carter was a false dawn. Judy Heumann, who like Eunice Fiorito, worked for Carter's presidential campaign, told reporters, "I was ashamed I helped Carter get elected."[9]

The times were changing. No single movement could stop the seemingly bipartisan neoliberal turn away from "the Great Society" placing limits on social policy under a regime of decentralization, deregulation, privatization, and austerity. New political realities made implementing rights difficult in part because rights were increasingly tied to spending and financial burdens. It also made it harder to get anything done when it came to expanding direct benefits which inherently involve overcoming budgetary hurdles in an era of cutbacks. By the middle of the first protest wave, activists increasingly responded to new levels of threat imposed by the Reagan administration that would eventually evolve into a more widespread neoliberal turn affecting states and local governments, especially when it came to budgetary politics and cost control.

In 1981 and 1982, more than half of all disability protests targeted the Reagan administration and congressional Republicans over proposed widespread budget cuts. Groups like the AFL-CIO, Sierra Club, National Education Association, Consumer Federation of America, National Council of Churches, and the Congressional Black Caucus along with 104 other organizations in March 1981 called for the "Nationwide Action for a Fair Budget." They received public support from some Democratic members of Congress. The protests included many people with disabilities fearing Congress-approved cuts would mean

---

[7] A Question of Access, *Washington Post*, March 15, 1988.

[8] Handicapped Protest High Court Ruling on Education, *Los Angeles Times*, August 18, 1979.

[9] HEW Offices Blocked to 20 Disabled Who Demand to Meet with Califano, *Cincinnati Enquirer*, April 23, 1977.

fewer opportunities and supports for disabled people especially in employment. Activists also pointed to how far-reaching the proposed federal cuts are and how they trickle down to local governments who rely on federal money to maintain services. Said one protester, "As I see it, the danger is coming from every direction – the city, the county, the state and the federal government."[10]

The first visible protest declined as new policy inroads were made in Congress. It was the beginning of a so-called golden age of federal disability policymaking (Pettinicchio 2019) seemingly bridging the end of wave one with the beginning of wave two. But by this time, federal rights policymaking and enforcement preoccupied activists and protesters far less than the complex and ambiguous ties between rights and direct benefits foreshadowed by an increasing call to end welfare as we knew it while emphasizing the "welfare-maximizing consequences of market exchange" (Abromovitz 2004; Evans and Sewell 2013, p. 36) This shift affected everything from transportation to social benefits, health, and education.

Several basic lessons emerged from the first disability protest wave: activist access to elite resources, threat, and retrenchment can coexist; areas of concern across different issues remain consistent resulting from some (often partial) victories, against a backdrop of new obstacles and challenges; visible and disruptive protests are effective at least some of the time; and as social movement efforts, protest shapes political culture even if it may not lead to immediate material gains. Importantly, the disability movement also reveals the generalized nature of threat as disability organizations grew more flexible in their strategies and worked with broader activist coalitions to counter sweeping structural changes – a precursor of sorts to the Resistance in the third wave of disability protest.

By the 1990s, in the early part of the second disability protest wave, 80 percent of visible protests revolved around transportation, social welfare, and healthcare issue areas. Activists turned their attention to spending cuts by state governments, which state officials often framed as a necessary response to federal government cutbacks, unfunded mandates, and efforts to balance budgets. Many of the social programs affected by cuts typically served the most marginalized communities seeing numerous protests across US states against cuts to mental health programs and programs specifically targeting people with disabilities.[11] This also came at a time when states like California, for example, were plagued by endless budget stalemates. In 1992 in Santa Ana, 250 disabled people protested budget cuts to programs helping people with developmental

---

[10] Marchers Protest Federal Cutbacks, *Los Angeles Times*, May 9, 1981.

[11] Mental-Health Budget Protest, *New York Times*, February 28, 1988; Protest over Chance of Disabled Aid Cuts, *San Francisco Chronicle*, June 22, 1990.

disabilities. As one protester told reporters, "We understand that almost every type of program is facing some kind of budget cut; that's no problem. But we need the Legislature and the governor to keep their promises and get this budget voted on."[12] As another protester stated, "I want everyone to know that this is a good program and I'm afraid I will end up living in the streets if the budget isn't passed."

Now armed with a great deal of experience in orchestrating visible protest events (as well as other more institutional activities), access to sympathetic elites, and ties to numerous organizations within and outside the disability rights movement, ADAPT took advantage of new political opportunities like Bill Clinton's focus on healthcare reform and bipartisan promises to address the homecare/institutionalization problem. In the early part of the second protest wave, the group was involved in almost every homecare-related protest – a trend that continued through the rest of the decade and into the 2000s. Homecare came to embody deep-seated structural disadvantage, institutionalized oppression and discrimination, and injustice. Although there were some gains including getting the issue on the policy agenda, opening serious talks, and developing policy proposals, not to mention the increased visibility of this long-time issue, little had been achieved in actually changing the system. Grievances remained unresolved, and activists continued to find new opportunities to make inroads, like for instance, in the 2016 presidential election.

Many grievances carried over into the third wave of visible disability protest; some of it the result of backsliding and some of it the institutional and cultural constraints that prevented interventions at all levels to address growing inequality and poverty among disabled Americans. Protests at the beginning of the third wave all dealt in some way with budgetary cutbacks and threats to existing benefits and services. Concerns over Medicaid and Social Security and the long-standing issue of the nursing home funding bias continued to fuel protests.

Veteran protest groups like DIA continued the transit accessibility fight. With regulations having long been in place, the focus was now on closing gaps in state and federal government regulations, especially as companies like Greyhound seemed to be working outside those rules. The third wave saw many of the same kinds of unresolved issues mobilize activists. But issue areas evolved alongside the movement. As such, the third wave also reflected a new reality whereby a much more experienced and well-seasoned disability movement had to contend with an ongoing dynamic between political opportunities and threat, and ongoing shifts in the elite-challenger relationship.

---

[12] Countywide Handicapped Protest Budget Stalemate, *Los Angeles Times*, August 12, 1992.

The federal government had become less relevant as a target of protest in the third wave even though in 2008, it enacted the ADA Restoration Act acknowledging over two decades of policy failures leaving Americans with disabilities in a life of precarity (Maroto and Pettinicchio 2014). For activists and organizations, the federal government had shown its limits in how far it would go to champion justice and equality for its citizens with disabilities. Perhaps in part for this reason, the disability movement began shifting its focus to challenging the more cultural underlying values and attitudes that support structural inequalities. The movement found success in addressing the negative, taken-for-granted ways everyday people think and talk about disability, as well as highlighting how entrenched those stereotypes are.

The focus on challenging norms and values that sustain inequality and systems of subordination and oppression has always been rooted in the activities of the disability rights movement, as it has been in other movements. But second wave protest, especially targeting the Muscular Dystrophy Association and the Jerry Lewis Telethons, set a new stage for activists and organizations in the third protest wave. Third wave protests directly targeted negative imagery and portrayals of disability focusing a great deal on pop culture representations of disability.

In 2007, Evelyn Ain, mother of a son with autism who attended a special learning center in Long Island New York, founded Autism United. Its inaugural walk in September alone raised over $150,000.[13] The following year, Autism United joined forces with Media Matters for America (an advocacy group working against conservative misinformation) to protest radio host Michael Savage's comments that children with autism are "brats who haven't been told to cut the act out." At the protest outside WOR station, with signs reading "Autism is no joke" and "Give Savage the pink slip," Autism United's executive director fired back saying "What he's doing is parroting what used to be said about autism 40 years ago, back in the heyday of Freudian analysis."[14] The Savage protests are an example of challenging toxic or offensive elements of popular culture presaging the "cancel" or "call-out culture" that exploded in the 2010s and early 2020s. While Savage stuck by his position, Autism United succeeded in getting sponsors like Aflac Insurance to back out.

The third wave of visible disability protests leading up to the Resistance illustrates how long-standing grievances are shaped by new norms and new politics. With each wave, movements see some gains in some areas whether partial, immediate, or long term, potentially offset by full or partial rollbacks in

---

[13] A Mother Fights for Autism Services, *New York Times*, November 18, 2007.

[14] Talk Radio Host Stands by His Remarks on Autism, *New York Times*, July 22, 2008.

others. With each iteration, activists face different sets of opportunities and threats, new allies and shifting relationships within and outside the cause field, different ways of framing issues and grievances, as well as diverse targets across the numerous issue areas activists work in. One could describe the cycle of contention in the disability cause field as "what was old is new again" but relying on this adage masks the continuity of grievances, activist networks, elite-movement relations, and the tentative nature of protest outcomes that keep activists involved in a movement over time and across issue areas.

When disability activists in the Resistance protested GOP efforts to repeal the Obama-era Affordable Care Act (ACA) in 2017, they were in fact fighting against a decades-old issue of institutionalization and lack of access to community-based care. TV personality Rachel Maddow on her MSNBC show paid brief tribute to ADAPT acknowledging the long history of the issue and of the activism surrounding it. She read aloud a quote from a news article from 1978:

> About 25 disabled persons seized two buses during Wednesday morning's downtown rush hour snarling traffic and daring police to make arrests. Quote: shortly after the 8:30 a.m. takeover, police arrived admitting they were not sure what to do. As police commanders came to assist on the scene, police officers decided not to arrest any of the handicapped protesters because, as one sergeant said, quote, we don't want to be the fall guys on this.

The protest Maddow referred to, however, is not in fact about homecare. It was an event organized in Denver by the "Gang of 19," a precursor to ADAPT (which was officially founded in 1983). About forty people in their wheelchairs blocked buses throughout most of the day accusing the Denver transit authority of "foot-dragging" when it came to making its buses accessible. "We Will Ride," protesters chanted, seen by many as the beginning of the disability rights movement in Denver.[15] Fast-forward forty years later, to 2018, when the Center for Independence of the Disabled sued the New York MTA over transit accessibility. Rise and Resist was there protesting at a press conference held on the day of the court hearing. "Accessibility is not a dismissible issue. It is not a luxury or convenience. It is a necessity and a civil right" proclaimed members of RAR. The long-time issue of accessible public transit was made salient again by the politics and mobilizing efforts of the Resistance. Similarly, extant grievances around inadequate healthcare and in-home care protest were punctuated by new threats from Trump and the GOP.

Disability activists and now Resisters took these long-standing issues and framed them within contemporary mobilization efforts against injustice and

---

[15] https://adapt.org/we-will-ride-the-gang-of-19/.

inequalities, cross-cutting movements and communities, emphasizing their interconnectedness. As one disabled activist put it:

> An important thing to point out is that disability rights intersects with [movements such as] gay rights, with black rights. Not every disabled person is a white man. I love the quote from Alice Wong: "My existence is resistance." That sums up how I feel. Just existing is a form of protest because people think disability is a dirty word. From the way we phrase things in society, to how the media represents us. People think it's the worst thing in the world to be disabled, and it's really not. It's not us that's the problem, it's the lack of access in society, the fact that things are not universally designed.[16]

The Resistance is a historical moment – an example of how longstanding concerns by the disability community were accentuated by new institutional and cultural realities. But the fact that threats are cross-cutting mobilizing coalitions of activists around issues that long predate them suggests a complicated dynamic between issue politics, mobilization, and social movement outcomes. If there is one key lesson the disability movement teaches us is that protest waves point to both processes of continuity and change; processes that are disjointed, non-recursive, and processes whose outcomes are fraught with ambiguity and uncertainty.

2 Protesting Long-Standing Grievances

Activists and organizations work within multiple intersecting issue areas important to their cause field. Social movement scholars have increasingly widened their lens to consider mobilization as embedded in a strategic action field (Fligstein and McAdam 2012; Pettinicchio 2013) – a field of actors inside and outside of social movements working toward common goals. This involves thinking about the institutional and cultural environments social movements inhabit, and the different issue areas a movement is engaged in (Bereni 2021). Cause fields emphasize the relationship between issue areas, the varieties of tactics and targets, and activists and organizations, within which to situate visible protest. Through this framework, protest can be seen as both a reason for, and outcome of, broader field changes (Meyer 2005, 2007).

Issue areas reflect complex intersections of grievances impacting people's daily lives. They are the intersecting spaces where movement mobilization occurs. For example, an individual with disabilities may not receive adequate educational resources to be competitive in the labor market and even if they are, they may not be able to get to work because they cannot access transportation. Additionally, without adequate social and health supports, individuals may

---

[16] www.thefader.com/2017/07/21/adapt-trumpcare-interview-protest-legislation.

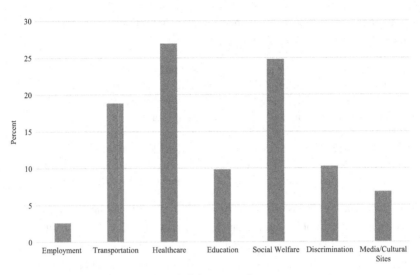

Figure 3 Disability visible protest issue areas (*n* = 234)

struggle to maintain good full-time jobs and adequate earnings (Pettinicchio and Maroto 2022). As Figure 3 shows, healthcare, social welfare, and transportation were the three most significant issues for visible protest overall, inhabited by the core grievances mobilizing disability activists since the movement's emergence.

Grievances alone may not generate protest but they are intricately linked to the ways in which issue politics and social movement mobilization coevolve (Almeida 2019; Amenta, Andrews and Caren 2019; Della Porta 2022; Oliver and Myers 2003). Access to elites, opportunities for different forms of collect-ive action, threat, and mobilizing structures – all of which play a part in turning grievances into action – are not static. Likewise, these ongoing efforts to effect change may not lead to desired outcomes, and even if they do, there is no guarantee that those gains will not be open to attack later on. Nixon's vetoes, Reagan's rights rollbacks and welfare retrenchment, and Trump's disregard for ADA enforcement and ACA repeal "suddenly" imposed grievances (Szasz 2007; Walsh, Warland, and Smith 1997) or at the very least, made them even more politically salient. Activists and groups found opportunities to respond, and with each protest cycle, resulted mainly in partial solutions and short-term victories, generating hope accompanied by long-term uncertainties.

With each protest wave, existing grievances take on new meaning as oppor-tunities facilitate mobilization when threats are present. Key disability issue areas like healthcare, social welfare, and transportation involved both victories and retrenchment, pointing to how the outcomes of protest are often partial leaving grievances unresolved. It sheds light on why and how issues remain open to future visible protest.

Protest waves are made up of disproportionate issue attention which also varies with time. This is in part a function of issue politics which can also act as an external force on mobilization (even though social movements in the long run can also shape issue politics). Issue areas experience successes and failures at different paces. Even though they may be facilitated or constrained by the same opportunities and threats, and rooted in overlapping organizational resources, efforts and outcomes in one issue area do not always translate to another issue area. Because protest waves consist of the combination of grievances, opportunities and resources tied to different (but often intersecting) issue areas with their own politics (Baumgartner and Jones 1993), attention paid to issues and grievances in each period will never be equal across areas movements simultaneously work within.

As Table 1 shows, healthcare, social welfare, and transportation together are key areas motivating protest in all three waves. Yet, while social welfare remains a consistently significant issue area across all three waves, transportation tapers off in the third wave, and healthcare comes to dominate the second and third waves. Discrimination declines significantly, while cultural sites and media grow from practically non-existent to 15 percent of all protests by the third wave. With transportation's decline, healthcare, education, and media/culture take up more of the share of visible protests in the third wave. All of this suggests a complex back-and-forth between endogenous forces like activist networks and SMOs, exogenous forces like issue politics, opportunities, and threats, and issue framing, strategy, goals, and outcomes that define the relationship between movements and their targets.

Protest waves reflect developments across a constellation of interrelated issues areas. Issue areas are dynamic contexts that motivate visible protest. Sometimes, multiple issue areas mobilize activists for similar reasons. Other

Table 1 Percent visible protest by issue area and wave (*n* = 234)

	Wave 1	Wave 2	Wave 3
Employment	2.9	1.0	3.4
Transportation	20.4	23.0	8.5
Healthcare	13.0	35.0	30.5
Education	7.2	7.0	16.9
Social Welfare	36.2	20.0	20.3
Discrimination	20.3	7.0	5.1
Media/Cultural Sites	0.0	7.0	15.3
	100	100	100

times, protests may be specific to developments within a particular issue space. It may very well be that some areas become a greater focus of protest activity, perhaps at the expense of others. But often, protests in one issue area can spill over into another, changing the circumstances around that issue. This perspective sheds light on both the continuity and distinctiveness of protest waves' internal dynamics (Koopmans 2004) and on how and why protest waves expand and decline. I examine three major issues areas of visible protest in greater detail below.

2.1 Social Welfare

The first sustained wave of visible disability protests began with Nixon's vetoing of the Rehabilitation Act. Eight other social welfare bills were on the chopping block as part of the early stages of "reforming" the welfare state. As one regional director of Health, Education, and Welfare put it, "Nixon vetoed the bill for economic reasons and because the implementation of the programs would have been in conflict with the aim of revenue sharing to decentralize many social services."[17] In November 1972, DIA demonstrated in Manhattan against the veto and in California, the Blind Action Committee protested at the Federal Building in Civic Center. Peter Leech of the Blind Action Committee said people with disabilities felt betrayed and that "many people who would have become more self-supporting with the aid of the bill will now have to remain on welfare at a cost to the taxpayers of millions of dollars."[18] By year's end, there was a general sense among those in the social welfare community including both federal and state-level officials that spending cuts would not solve what many in the early 1970s saw as a "horrendous welfare mess."[19]

Throughout the rest of the 1970s, social welfare–related protests increasingly targeted state governments as governors sought to rein in spending. This, of course, impacted an array of intersecting issues: income supports, healthcare, generalized resources to people with intellectual and developmental disabilities, mainstream and special education, and adequate and affordable housing. People were simply "outraged by budget cuts."[20] Directed at California Governor Brown, activists, many of whom included parents of children with disabilities, and presaging the Medicaid nursing home fight, argued that cuts to community-based social services means having to send disabled people into more costly institutions. A year late in 1980, activists protested a proposal in the California

---

[17] Disabled Protest Aid Veto, *San Francisco Examiner*, November 7, 1972.

[18] Disabled Protest Aid Veto, *San Francisco Examiner*, November 7, 1972.

[19] Wrong Approach to Welfare Reform, *Pittsburgh Post-Gazette*, December 18, 1972.

[20] Disabled Outraged by Budget Cuts, *Los Angeles Times*, March 3, 1979.

legislature that would eliminate automatic cost of living increases for people with disabilities under SSI.[21]

In 1981 and 1982, groups representing different communities came together to rally against the Reagan administration which turned out to be a unifying target among activists across cause fields. In April 1981, a massive "Survival Rally" was held in Los Angeles by more than 100 groups protesting Reagan cutbacks on programs that help the most vulnerable people.[22] Just a month later, after the House approved Reagan's budget cuts, protesters representing religious communities, labor unions, the Congressional Black Caucus, Sierra Club, and a host of community groups including disability and elderly groups chanted "Let them eat jellybeans"[23] – Reagan's favorite candy. As part of the National Days of Resistance protest campaign, thousands of demonstrators in May 1982 organized by the All People's Congress (APC) – a coalition of student, labor, and community groups – protested against "Roll Back Reaganism." According to reports, the coalition of activists at the protest was diverse ranging "in age from about 15 to 65, included representatives of American Indians, Blacks, poor people, the handicapped, homosexuals and Haitian immigrants."[24] Larry Holmes, a cofounder of the APC said that "they will keep the pressure on" and that the "marchers were united by opposition to the Reagan administration."[25]

As early as 1981, the threat of spending and program cuts was becoming more pervasive as it trickled down to the state and local levels. In September 1981, about 1,000 people protested Congress and Reagan in Washington, DC, as part of the Disabled Americans Freedom Rally.[26] Activists feared that conversion of federal grants into fixed state block grants would mean reduced funding to housing, educational, and job programs as states would absorb higher costs during economic downturn coupled with higher costs of living. This led state governors to propose cuts to programs as they are typically more reluctant to propose higher taxes to close budget gaps. It posed significant challenges for disability programs in the 1990s as well, reflected in the second wave of visible protests. As one Howard University law student participating in the protest explained, it is the federal government "wiping its hands of responsibility" shifting the burden to states. Funds meant to provide accessible housing has dried up and as one protester explained, "we have to compete with the elderly for housing."[27] Another protester described

---

[21] Welfare Protest Staged Near Senator's Office, *Los Angeles Times*, December 25, 1980.

[22] Rally Protests Aid Cuts, *Los Angeles Times*, April 2, 1981.

[23] Marchers Protest Federal Cutbacks, *Los Angeles Times*, May 9, 1981

[24] Marchers Protest against Reagan Policies, *Washington Post*, May 2, 1982.

[25] Marchers Protest against Reagan Policies, *Washington Post*, May 2, 1982.

[26] Physically Handicapped Protest Cuts in Services, *Washington Post*, September 10, 1981.

[27] Physically Handicapped Protest Cuts in Services, *Washington Post*, September 10, 1981.

these attacks as coming from narrow-minded people who are only temporarily "able- bodied" and they too will eventually be affected by these cuts.

For protesters, state responses were seen as trying to "out Reagan Reagan."[28] In Sacramento, a coalition of seniors, disabled people, those representing the poor, and other community groups protested the state's cutbacks and scrapping the consumer price index to determine costs of living increases. In the late-1980s, activists, mostly from NARC, protested one of Maryland Governor Schaefer's many cost-saving measures: charge parents of developmentally disabled children fees for state services, including those in state-run group homes. Schaefer's reply was that "the bottom line is the concept" and the plan was meant to shift responsibility onto families rather than expensive state institutions.[29] As an issue area, social welfare contributed to the second and third protest waves in large part because opportunities around Social Security reform were coupled with threats to disability programs whether Reagan-era cutbacks or Clinton-era "welfare reform," seeping into state budgetary politics.

For years in California, budget stalemates jeopardized the provision of services targeting mental health and disability. Like in other states, the governor's office and legislature were focused on deficit reduction avoiding any discussion of raising taxes. So problematic, California government officials created a commission to investigate implementation of these services and sought consultation from community groups.[30] Throughout the second protest wave, these budgetary politics would endanger vulnerable Americans. Over 500 people demonstrated at the State Building in San Francisco in June 1990 when Governor Deukmajian proposed keeping funding for disability programs at last year's levels.[31] Just a week later, protesters were removed from the governor's office outraged by proposals to cut independent living programs.[32] Another California budget stalemate in 1992 mobilized over 250 people seeking to get the budget voted in. Twenty programs in Orange County helping developmentally disabled people risked closing potentially leaving some homeless.[33] The California legislature and Governor Pete Wilson failed to pass a budget by

---

[28] Seniors March to Protest Aid Cuts, *Los Angeles Times*, March 5, 1981.

[29] Md. Parents Storm Hearing to Protest Fees for Care of Retarded Adults, *Washington Post*, February 10, 1989.

[30] Vote by GOP Protested / Bay Area Disability Centers in Peril, *San Francisco Chronicle*, February 23, 1989.

[31] Protest over Chance of Disabled Aid Cuts, *San Francisco Chronicle*, June 22, 1990.

[32] Disabled Protesters Removed from Governor's Office, *San Francisco Chronicle*, June 29, 1990.

[33] Countywide Handicapped Protest Budget Stalemate, *Los Angeles Times*, August 12, 1992.

the constitutional deadline. They finally passed a budget, but critics still called for further austerity. In Washington, DC, Clinton's welfare reform led to further local cuts to social programs. The Fair Budget Coalition organized a demonstration which turned out 200 people affected by a wide array of cuts, whether drug treatment programs, homeless subsidies, daycare services, or home aide services.[34]

Many of these protests could not stop the kinds of cuts proposed by legislators. Local and state officials used the "unfunded mandate" to justify their retrenchment efforts. Unfunded mandates refer to laws passed by the federal government ranging from the Clean Air Act to the Americans with Disabilities Act which leave the costs of enforcement up to state and local governments. Clinton responded to protests by mayors and governors[35] by passing an executive order requiring federal officials to consult with local officials on unfunded mandates. Some environmental groups grew concerned that the unfunded mandate would lead to abolishing programs and have a "chilling effect" on future policy, a concern no doubt shared by those in the social welfare community as well.

By the end of the decade, social welfare–related protests especially around cutbacks had subsided. They would re-resurface in the late-2000s around social service cuts. In 2011, California Governor Jerry Brown appealed to five GOP state senators whose votes he needed to get the budget passed. The five hold outs had a new set of demands including pension rollbacks and further restrictions on state spending. Protesters carried signs reading "C-Me as a person not a budget" and "Please don't cut our services we receive."[36] A few months later, upon learning that the state had closed some of the budget gaps,[37] the California Partnership – a coalition of local activist groups – demonstrated against welfare cuts and cuts to cash grants for elderly and disabled people. California lawmakers ultimately approved a 2012 budget a few months later that included a host of cutbacks to education, care worker pay, and about 100 million in cuts to services for developmentally disabled people. Groups took the cuts to court and a federal judge issued a temporary order against these.

Social welfare–related visible protests, many motivated by threat, illustrate some of the hurdles involved in preventing rollbacks, continuity in grievances and issue politics, and the complex nature of social movement outcomes, which are often partial and potentially ephemeral.

---

[34] Protesters Try to 'Teach' Control Board a Lesson: About 200 Turn Out for Rally against Social Spending Cuts, *Washington Post*, May 16, 1997.

[35] Costly Federal Mandates Spur Protest: States, Counties Seek Relief from Programs Imposed without Funding, *Washington Post*, October 27, 1993.

[36] 5 GOP Senators Say Brown Budget Talks Have Stalled, *Los Angeles Times*, March 8, 2011.

[37] $6.6-billion windfall aids budget plan, *Los Angeles Times*, May 17, 2011.

Throughout the 1980s, nonprofit organizations, SMOs, and activist networks were also undergoing important changes chief among them a stronger focus on political advocacy and a hybrid service-advocacy model (Minkoff 2002). By the 1990s, there were fewer disability groups being formed and an increase in the number of existing groups folding (Pettinicchio 2019). This led to a reorganization of resources and strategy. But groups continued to rely on disruptive tactics like visible protest which had become a key part of the disability movement's tactical repertoire. Early protest groups like DIA and ADAPT made a long-lasting impact on the disability organizational sector. Not only did these groups work to expand the disability constituency, but they were also critical for maintaining interest in ongoing inequalities and disadvantage, framing these as threats and attacks on disability itself.

Even with overall organizational decline, the 1990s and 2000s saw a proliferation of autism organizations. Groups like DC Autism Parents and Autism United founded in the late 2000s, learned from the direct action and visible protests of groups like DIA, ACCD, and ADAPT. These groups worked to expand autism services and programs and to protect existing programs from retrenchment including in education (like Individualized Education Programs or IEPs). These groups sought to distinguish themselves from established groups like the Autism Society of America founded in the 1960s, much like DIA did in the 1970s from the established groups of that time.

In 2006, the Autistic Self-Advocacy Network (ASAN) was founded which unlike parent-led groups, was run for and by autistic people (see Carey, Block, and Scotch 2020). The group also worked toward educational mainstreaming, while bringing its message of inclusion and economic injustice into other areas. For example, the group targeted the legal practice of assigning subminimum wages to workers with disabilities (Maroto and Pettinicchio 2022), linking it to the broader living wage movement and coordinating protests in different cities.[38]

By the late 2010s, autism organizations increasingly focused on the inequalities surrounding access to autism programs and services based on "race and money."[39] In 2019, Maria Davis-Pierre, self-advocate and mother of two autistic children created Autism in Black, Inc. In 2020, the ASAN joined forces with the NAACP and other groups to oppose a Senate policing bill. In Pittsburgh, Black Autistic Lives Matter continued to raise awareness around delayed diagnosis of autism among Black children, a practice which excludes Black children from receiving critical social provisions.[40]

---

[38] Slave Wages for the Disabled, *The Daily Beast*, September 23, 2015.
[39] Autism on Long Island Race and Money, *Newsday*, January 11, 2008.
[40] Black autistic lives matter, *New Pittsburgh Courier*, June 8, 2022.

Like the protests of the early 1980s, the third protest wave brought social welfare for people with disabilities into a larger conversation around inequalities, marginalization, and economic injustice. Contemporary activist efforts associated with Occupy, BLM, and the Resistance, helped reinvigorate issues and introduce them to a new generation of activists. Healthcare too would re-emerge as an issue of intersectional injustice, shaped by new issue politics but also a familiar mix of opportunities and threats.

2.2 Healthcare

There have been over fifty attempts by Republicans to undermine provisions of the Affordable Care Act. They came very close to doing so in the summer of 2017. These frequent rollback attempts left some of the most vulnerable Americans including low-income people, women, and people of color in a constant state of precarity. This was nothing new for people with disabilities for whom care was not just a matter of accessing services, but a matter of rights, illustrating how distinct issue areas can intersect within a cause field (see Pettinicchio 2023 on the welfare-rights connection).

In June 2017, ADAPT along with other long-time disability groups including NARC and Easter Seals held a protest at Leader Mitch McConnell's office against the Republican bill threatening to cut funding to home-based care which would require placing people into care facilities. An estimated 40–60 people were arrested and dragged out of the building garnering a great deal of national media attention. The following month, MoveOn.org, Our Revolution, Indivisible, and CREDO came together to protest repeal-and-replace of ACA. Their goal was to ensure that senators who promised they would not vote for the GOP Better Care Reconciliation Act stuck to their word. The July National Day of Protest was meant to call them out in the most visible way possible.[41] Right-wing TV personality, Sean Hannity, called this broad coalition of activists "left wing agitators."

For long-time activists, the fight over the 2017 healthcare bill was a fight they had been waging for years in their efforts to change Medicaid funding which biases nursing home care. The events of 2017 had an important impact on mobilization inside and outside of the disability rights movement. As one journalist described, "like many of the protesters galvanized after the presidential election, the first half of 2017 has been something of a crash course in activism and healthcare policy ... "[42] It brought in new disability activists, shed

---

[41] Health-Care Activists Plan to Make GOP's July 4 Hell, *The Daily Beast*, June 29, 2017.
[42] For health-care activists, Senate bill's tabling is no excuse to rest, *TCA Regional News*, July 2, 2017.

light on the intersectional and far-reaching impacts of care, and raised the profile of a decades-old core disability issue area among voters and policy-makers. Now more than ever, activists emphasized that the effects of these regressive healthcare policies are not limited to people with disabilities.[43] They tied long-time grievances around nursing homes to evolving issue politics like healthcare reform, much like they had in the 1990s, finding new opportunities to challenge threats.

Healthcare illustrates the interplay between issue politics and mobilization as both coevolved creating and constraining opportunities for change. As an issue area for disability, healthcare was not always so exclusively tied to the home care/nursing home fight. In fact, the first protest wave mostly focused attention around aging, health for people with developmental disabilities, and black lung among miners. Healthcare during the second protest wave began with protests around cuts to healthcare and mental health-related services, as well as HIV/AIDS. Much of these protests faced similar challenges as those targeting social welfare more generally because they were directly tied to spending.

Healthcare evolved during that second wave especially when ADAPT turned its focus to homecare in the 1990s, and when new structural opportunities surfaced around the potential for major healthcare reforms. Not surprisingly, 56 percent of all healthcare-related protests took place during that second protest wave. The focus would increasingly shift toward the nursing home/homecare fight. Of the thirty-four protests around healthcare during the second protest wave, 71 percent specifically focused on the homecare fight.

ADAPT, which was in 1989 still being referred to as Americans Disabled for *Accessible Public Transit*, targeted deplorable conditions in nursing homes in one of the earliest nursing home care protests. Americans Disabled for Accessible Public Transit protesters held a vigil at Judge David M. Schacter's home. Schacter had overturned a jury award to a woman sexually assaulted in a nursing home.[44] 1991 is an important year in the healthcare issue area as it saw numerous visible protests across different cities targeting a variety of institutions and organizations. Healthcare protests were becoming singularly focused on the nursing home bias making explicit links to Medicaid spending. In Baltimore, 300 demonstrators protested the Health Care and Financing Administration demanding a Medicaid funding shift favoring homecare.[45] Shortly thereafter, at another demonstration organized by ADAPT and led by one of its leaders, Mike Auberger, protesters "threw themselves from their wheelchairs and wriggled toward a barricade of police cars." Some formed

---

[43] People who have everything to lose, *The Burlington Free Press*, July 7, 2017.

[44] Activists for Handicapped Protest at Judge's Home, *Los Angeles Times*, December 21, 1989.

[45] Disabled Demonstrate for More Aid, *Washington Post*, April 30, 1991.

a chain to block access to the Department of Health and Human Services. In Florida, ADAPT protesters reportedly smashed police cars with wheelchairs and blocked a hotel entrance where nursing home representatives were meeting.

By now, ADAPT had developed a reputation inside and outside the movement – these article titles say it all – "Militant Advocacy Group for Disabled Revels in Role as Agitator" and "Disabled Militants Protest at Capitol To Live on Their Own." One report described ADAPT as using "wheelchairs to barricade buildings, and members crawl across dirty streets to dramatize the helplessness of people in nursing homes."[46]

Throughout this second wave of protest, the use of human blockades had become part of the disability movement's tactical repertoire. In a 1992 Maryland protest, activists framed homecare access as a class-based issue – it was only one of three Medicaid programs slated to be entirely eliminated – a program mostly helping the poorest.[47] ADAPT vowed to hold protests in all state capitals like the one in Arkansas targeting then Governor Bill Clinton. As ADAPT president Terry Winkler stated, "We'd like to give notice to all Democratic candidates, to all Democrats and Republicans, that this issue is one you're going to have to deal with."[48]

Activists then saw an opportunity to bring the issue back to Clinton when he ran for president. They turned the cost frame which had been used against the disability cause on its head. Activists argued that it is cheaper to pay for homecare than expensive institutionalized care and that attendant workers need to be better compensated. With Clinton in the White House, activists saw new opportunities to reform Social Security and Healthcare.[49] But like social welfare, states looking to trim budgets often targeted homecare because unlike nursing home care, which is an entitlement under federal law, homecare is not. Here too, the problem of perceived cost, spending, and major policy overhauls acted as significant structural barriers for activists to achieve their goals.

At first, the mid-90s reflected new political opportunities for policy reform – a potential for significant institutional change around homecare. A sympathetic president was in power, and Republican Speaker of the House, Newt Gingrich, supported MICASA, a proposed law that would amend the Social Security Act to address the nursing home funding bias. ADAPT put pressure on leaders to ensure people with disabilities had

---

[46] Disabled Protesters Disrupt Capitol, *Washington Post*, May 11, 1993.

[47] Threat to Program for Disabled Poor Sparks Md. Protest, *Washington Post*, September 29, 1992.

[48] Disabled Protesters Occupy Clinton's Office, *Washington Post*, January 1, 1992.

[49] Protesters in Wheelchairs Block Clinton Headquarters in S.F., *San Francisco Chronicle*, October 20, 1992.

a seat at the table. Meanwhile, protests in the mid-to-late-90s continued to target nursing homes and the nursing home lobby group. In 1997, 350 people participated in a sit-in before the Rayburn House Office Building demanding a hearing be set regarding MICASA.[50] The proposed law went nowhere despite bipartisan support. In 1998, activists again turned to disruptive protests, but the issue remained unresolved. Although the 1999 Olmstead Supreme Court case, which ruled that needless institutionalization is discrimination, gave activists and advocates of homecare new ammunition, it seemed to do little to address the broader political problem of Medicaid funding.

Protesters felt let down by federal policymakers. They continued their demonstrations focusing more on states and organizations rather than the federal government. In 2000, several hundred ADAPT members held a sit-in at the American Medical Association and Andrew Cuomo's office – Cuomo was then HUD Secretary. After both agreed to meet with ADAPT, Auberger said, "both of these targets make quite a sweet victory." They also targeted Cuomo's home "to make it a little more personal."[51] As governor of New York, Cuomo would once again face demonstrators when he proposed to cut homecare as a response to Trump and Republican threats to reduce federal healthcare spending. It would be an ongoing battle across the country. In 2002, activists protested California Governor Gray's budget cuts.[52] They wanted an assembly bill that directly promotes reductions in the number of disabled people in institutions. As one activist said, "We're trying to stimulate conversation." Over the next several years, they would target Governor Arnold Schwarzenegger worried about "the beginning of the dismantling of the safety net that has protected disabled people." ADAPT also continued to highlight poor conditions in nursing homes and in 2003, holding banners that read, "Stolen Lives," and forming human barricades, targeted the Justice Department demanding a thorough investigation of several nursing homes.

The 2000s saw numerous policy efforts to address the issue, including Money Follows the Person and Promoting Wellness for Individuals with Disabilities Act in 2006 and 2007, and the Community Choice Act (2007–2009). All these efforts died. Additionally, in the 2000s, only about half of all states had some program under Medicaid that provided homecare.

With the Community Choice Act stalled, ADAPT organized a demonstration in 2007 of over 500 people who descended on the Capitol. During the early part

---

[50] Disabled Hold Protest on Capitol Hill, *Washington Post*, November 11, 1997 and Hearing Sought on Bill to Aid Home Care, *Washington Post*, November 11, 1997.

[51] Disability Group Makes Point – Demonstrations at AMA and Cuomo's Home Spur Meetings, *Washington Post*, June 20, 2000.

[52] Ventura County; Disabled Protest Proposed Cutbacks, *Los Angeles Times*, April 18, 2002.

of the third protest wave, disability activists emphasized that homecare is an issue at the intersection of race, class, and disability. This helped as the issue gained traction with other constituencies. In 2008, the NAACP and the National Organization for Women (NOW) participated in congressional hearings alongside ADAPT on the issue of homecare. In 2009, ADAPT held another protest around the Community Choice Act. Apparently, "ADAPT spokesman Tim Wheat said members of the group met earlier in the day with Nancy DeParle, director of the White House Office of Health Care Reform, to discuss health care reform but left dissatisfied."[53] In 2012, ADAPT reached new levels of public notoriety when at one of its protests, celebrity Noah Wiley (of the TV show ER) was arrested along with ADAPT members who cuffed themselves to the rotunda in the Cannon House Office Building.[54] If it was not going to get policy change, ADAPT would certainly work to raise widespread support for healthcare reform and forge ties with other constituencies.

By 2017, activists helped revive direct action within the disability community in the context of Trump's presidency, the Women's March, and the American Resistance, while recognizing the long and bumpy road ADAPT and others traveled to get to this point.[55] They raised the salience of the issue and formed important alliances with other cause fields. The National Women's Health Network's Raising Women's Voices campaign strongly advocated for protection of ACA and early on emphasized issues of race, disability, and class in connecting it to the Women's March. Motivated by a sense of growing antagonism from a "hostile" Congress and administration,[56] they along with ACT UP and ADAPT focused on issues like Medicaid waivers which had direct bearing on people with disabilities seeking community-based care.

Like social welfare, healthcare illustrates how grievances affecting a community interact with political developments that also cut across issue areas and constituencies. It points to how opportunity and threat, organizational resources, and the outcomes of mobilization go on to shape the ebb and flow of protest.

2.3 Transportation

Public transportation too is a cross-cutting issue. People with disabilities, elderly people, low-income people, people of color, and immigrants disproportionately rely on public transit to get around. The disability rights movement did

---

[53] More Than 100 Arrested in Series of Protests, *Washington Post*, April 28, 2009.

[54] rs-celebvocate24, *Washington Post*, April 24, 2012.

[55] These Americans Helped Save Health Care. Don't Forget Them Now, *New York Times*, September 23, 2021.

[56] https://nwhn.org/nwhn-action-januaryfebruary-2017/.

much to push the framing of transit accessibility as both an economic and civil rights matter very early on. It is an issue area that has seen some concrete gains – from kneeling buses to accessible transit stations. Yet, visible protests in transit also experienced failed and/or ambiguous long-term outcomes. Early protests were a lesson to activists that when push came to shove on perceived cost, austerity measures tended to win out.

Nonetheless, transit-related disability protests were among the most disruptive, notable, and attention drawing. Perhaps this is why disability movement leaders from Auberger of ADAPT to Judy Heumann pointed to the success of these visible protests given their broader symbolic meaning for the movement even if they did not always lead to material gains.

Following legislative momentum in Congress like the Architectural Barriers Act of 1968 and the 1970 Urban Mass Transportation Act (Katzmann 1986; Pettinicchio 2012, 2013, 2017; Pettinicchio 2019) which signaled important political opportunities for equal access, Heumann and DIA "broke a tradition of silent suffering" when in 1970, they picketed New York city hall for expensive and inadequate transportation – the organization's "first militant move."[57] Congress put pressure on transit authorities receiving federal monies to make their systems accessible. Transit authorities and their lobby group, APTA, fought back, threatening to undo this legislative progress.

Protest directly resulted in both short-term and long-term gains. For example, transportation secretary Brock Adams who was also pressured by a lawsuit filed by twelve disability groups, proclaimed that all buses purchased after 1979 using federal funds would have to be accessible. The transit industry saw new rights regulations as burdens "imposed" onto them suggesting they would not comply. Social movement groups and activists reacted to those threats. By the late-1970s, DIA and the ACCD were joined by the Gang of 19 (who would become ADAPT) creating an important organizational base to help sustain visible protest in transportation.

By the second protest wave, two-thirds of transit-related protests were associated with ADAPT. These were generally very disruptive and purposely attention-grabbing. In 1984, ADAPT protesters "captured" seven buses by leaning on them with crutches or laying down on the street in front of them. ADAPT demanded and got a meeting with the DC transit general manager about equipping all buses with wheelchair lifts. ADAPT also planned to take their demands to APTA – one of their chief targets.[58] And they did just that. A few days later, fifteen protesters blocked a bus in front of the hotel where

---

[57] Disabled organize to fight for rights, *Newsday*, August 23, 1971.

[58] Buses 'Captured' in Demonstration by Handicapped, *Washington Post*, September 28, 1984.

APTA was holding a meeting.[59] Visible protests in public transit became a key tool in raising public awareness around public transit inaccessibility.

Although other groups like DIA, Disgruntled Advocates of Marin, Communities Actively Living Independent & Free, Alameda County Coalition for Accessible Transportation, and National Federation of the Blind engaged in transit protests, ADAPT became a national symbol of disability rights militancy. It held protests across the country, in Cincinnati, Denver Atlanta, LA, New York, DC, San Francisco, Dallas, Louisville, and in many other cities.

As more local transit authorities made their systems accessible and local transit advocacy groups kept vigil, ADAPT refocused their attention on private charter bus companies like Greyhound. One of the earliest of these protests was in 1985 when twenty protesters blocked a Trailways bus at an LA terminal. Although they made gains with local transit authorities, private bus operators still required wheelchairs be folded when brought on board. Wade Blank, one of the protest organizers said "We don't think a person should have to be carried aboard a bus ... It's very dehumanizing .... They're taking away their legs."[60] Protesters demanded new legislation to address companies like Trailways and Greyhound. All the while, ADAPT understood that if they were to shape legislative change, they would also have to maintain regular channels with political elites, and so the group would continue to testify at congressional hearings while engaging in visible disruptive protests.

Despite more institutional tactics and meetings with officials, Blank and Auberger acknowledged that visible protests like this one were important in drawing broader attention to the issue. Blank said, "This is a symbolic protest, just like the civil rights protests of the 60s." In 1988, numerous protests targeted Greyhound across the United States. In LA, protesters accused Greyhound of "flagrant violation of California's access laws."[61] In Dallas, several protesters were arrested for blocking passengers from boarding onto Greyhound buses at the terminal.[62] The following year, twenty of the over 200 demonstrators in Atlanta were arrested for blocking Greyhound-Trailway buses. Protesters placed their wheelchairs in front of buses, some chaining themselves to the bus steering wheel. One protester said, "I am trying to hold up Greyhound because they are holding up my life." Auberger purposely targeted Greyhound-Trailways because the company continued to use cost as reason for delaying

---

[59] Disabled Protesters Block Bus at Transit Meeting Site, *Washington Post*, October 1, 1984.

[60] Disabled People Block Bus at Terminal, *Los Angeles Times*, February 10, 1985.

[61] Bus Protest Stops Traffic Disabled Group Wants Access on Greyhound, *Los Angeles Times*, August 13, 1988.

[62] Wheelchair Users Arrested in Protests at Bus Stations, *New York Times*, September 7, 1988.

making their buses accessible. In addition to protesting at local bus terminals, ADAPT simultaneously protested at federal government offices for not doing more on accessible public transit.[63]

The 1990s saw a decline in transit-related protests in part because ADAPT refocused its efforts on nursing homes and the Medicaid funding bias. There were continued protests targeting private bus operators. In the late 1990s, toward the end of the second wave of protest, two of the last ADAPT organized transit protests took place, one coorganized with DIA. Now armed with the ADA, protesters in New York, San Diego, and Los Angeles charged Greyhound for not complying with the law. However, the response from Greyhound continued to be that there are no federal regulations specifically applying to private operators and that disabled people can book ahead of time and have a Greyhound employee carry passengers onto the bus. This of course was unsatisfactory and is not what activists understood accessibility to mean. DIA protesters reminded people that disabled people are more likely to rely on buses than air travel and trains because they have lower incomes.[64]

The early part of the third disability protest wave saw relatively few protests focus on transit. Much of those protests dealt with the perennial issue of fare hikes targeting local governments. They drew from protests of the early 1980s when the Citizens Advisory committee on Accessible Transportation and the Agency on Aging, Legal Aid Foundation of LA, and the Coalition for Economic Survival – a multi-racial and multi-ethnic grassroots community group – came together on this exact issue. The coalition would also file a lawsuit. Although equal access to public transit was framed as a matter of rights, when it came to fare hikes, disability groups and activists faced similar obstacles much like they did with healthcare and social welfare under an austerity regime. Yet, activists continued to raise awareness about the class, ageist, gendered, racial, and ableist aspects around fare hikes and access.[65] Now, with RAR and the Elevator Action Group which drew from BLM and the Resistance to raise awareness about injustice associated with transit, the issue saw some new life albeit shakier and less sustained. Transit protests illustrate how long-term grievances remain on the public agenda like accessible transit stations and fare hikes. They also highlight the many partial successes in the short-term, as well as some long-term successes – from accessible buses to raising awareness about inequality.

---

[63] 25 Disabled People Held in Atlanta Bus Protest, *New York Times*, September 29, 1989.

[64] Disrupting Sales at Greyhound, Disabled Protest Bus Access, *New York Times*, August 9, 1997.

[65] Speakers Protest Metro Board Proposal to Raise Rates for Elderly, Handicapped, *Washington Post*, January 28, 1983.

2.4 The Targets of Visible Protest

Issue areas reflect a dance between gains and losses which uncoincidentally overlap with the ebb and flow of visible protest. Favorable political opportunities may motivate visible protest but so too does the sense that progress hits a wall. Experiencing losses and repeated let downs endemic to virtually all issue areas explored in this volume and often the result of broader exogenous forces – that is, forces outside the disability movement – motivated intense disruptive protest (Meyer and Minkoff 2004; Snow et al. 1998) whether efforts at the local, state, or federal levels. Activists and organizations react to a hybrid of opportunity and threat (McAdam et al. 2010). As Van Dyke and Soule (2002) and Almeida (2019) explain, threat can signal loss, an erosion of influence, and longer-term disadvantages for movement groups and activists.

Social welfare, healthcare, and transportation are large complex issues that not only cut across policy silos but also affect many diverse constituencies. Given their complexity, activists seeking to effect change targeted federal, state, and local governments, as well as firms, organizations, and businesses. Yet, the distribution of targets is not even across space (see Table 2) or time (see Figure 4). Targets of visible protest across issue spaces vary because some targets are inherently more closely tied to some issues over others. When those issues dominate, movement organizations and activists direct their attention to those meaningful targets. Over time, political opportunities shift, issues may get partially resolved at one level but remain open at other levels. For example, the passage of disability laws was followed by weak

Table 2 Percent visible protest targets by issue area ($n = 234$)

| Issue Areas | Target | | | |
	Federal	State	Local	Businesses/ Organizations
Employment	2.6	2.0	1.9	3.8
Transportation	5.2	2.0	37.0	36.5
Healthcare	35.1	37.3	16.7	15.4
Education	7.8	0.0	24.1	7.7
Social Welfare	24.7	52.9	14.8	7.7
Discrimination	22.1	5.9	3.7	3.8
Media/Cultural Sites	2.6	0.0	1.9	25.0
	100 (77)	100 (51)	100 (54)	100 (52)

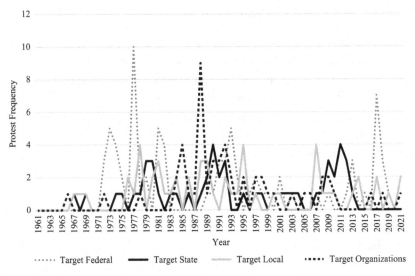

Figure 4 Visible protest targets over time

enforcement with many veto points facilitating retrenchment. Similarly, the federal government's inability to reform Medicaid in the homecare fight explains in part why groups focused on state targets instead. And so, we would expect shifts in targets of visible protest across waves as well.

Rights and discrimination-related protests mostly targeted the federal government which makes sense given that from its inception, rights-based protests were tied to policy developments at the federal level. On the other hand, education-related protests mostly targeted state government, and protests around media, representation, and culture mostly targeted businesses and organizations. And although there were federal mandates requiring local authorities to comply with transit accessibility, transportation-related protests mainly targeted local governments and organizations because they pushed back against regulations. Local authorities were also seen as more proximate targets, especially when it seemed the federal government did all it was going to do policy wise.

Conversely, healthcare-related protests consistently targeted both federal and state governments given how threats of retrenchment were playing out. Yet, a significant number also targeted local governments and organizations (e.g., nursing homes and their lobby group). This issue demonstrates the multipronged approach movement organizations like ADAPT engage in on complicated social issues. It also showcases ADAPT's flexibility across issues and its ability to narrow in on different targets relevant to the group's objectives.

Targets are a function of issue area jurisdictions, political opportunities, and beliefs among activists that these targets have some influence in resolving their grievances. As issues evolve, targets also shift. The federal government was a significant target of visible protest during the first wave in part driven by the focus on discrimination and social welfare. During the second wave, the federal government became less of a target of protest as businesses and organizations took center stage. This in large part reflects the growing focus on transit accessibility. State governments become a more prominent target in the second wave driven by budget cuts and state deficit reduction strategies. The federal government would only regain relevance as a target in the latter part of the second wave, driven by new political opportunities around healthcare reform.

At different points throughout the third protest wave, there is a resurgence in federal, state, and to a lesser extent local governments as targets. The spike in local targets is a mix of three developments: cuts to local disability-related programs, transit protests around fares and access, and cuts to educational programs. The rise in state targets is a result of proposed budget cuts in both healthcare and social welfare. Finally, in the years leading up to the Resistance, the federal government increasingly became a focus of visible protest after a period of relative absence. These mainly were about veteran's benefits as well as potential threats to social welfare and healthcare by the Obama administration. Then, Trump and McConnell re-invigorated protesters, as did other members of his administration, including Education Secretary Betsy DeVos. DeVos' budget saw major cutbacks to programs for students with disabilities.

Through each wave, issues were transformed by activism, and activism shaped subsequent protest motivated by new social, cultural, economic, and political conditions. In each wave, threats from targets unified a diverse group of protesters within the disability community and other affinity groups. Targets also reveal what kinds of relationships constituencies, activists, and different organizations have with elites – sometimes supportive, other times more antagonistic. Activists develop ties with governments and other organizations, especially given their protracted engagement in multiple issue areas over time. Even some of the most militant groups engaging in disruptive visible protests worked routinely with the targets they were protesting.[66] The "civil rights counterrevolution" ushered in by the Reagan administration brought civil rights movement communities closer together around this broad threat. The AFL-CIO, NOW, National Women's Law Center, Leadership Conference on Civil Rights, National Urban League, and the NAACP joined disability groups as they participated in congressional hearings. A similar dynamic unfolded around healthcare which also galvanized different communities engaging in both institutional and more disruptive visible tactics.

---

[66] Disabled Protest Reagan Plan, *New York Times*, May 1, 1982.

3 "Spread the Word" about Inclusion

Visible protests are, by definition, widely seen. They are attention-grabbing on purpose sending a message that extends beyond their direct targets of action. Visible protests, regardless of issue space – from social welfare to education to media representations – have been critical in publicizing grievances and goals, hoping that these would do more to encourage not only structural change, but cultural change as well. Changing hearts and minds in addition to (or instead of) focusing on specific material gains may be more advantageous if activists encounter insurmountable obstacles with the latter (like influencing policy). Changing the culture could have longer-term positive impacts facilitating material changes as more conscience constituents (and voters) become aware of inequalities and injustice. While visible protests targeting popular culture tend to generate a lot of attention, their outcomes face similar constraints as other protests especially in terms of whether victories have lasting power down the road.

Like many historically marginalized groups, disability representation in print and video media has often been negative, stereotypical, or non-existent (Foster and Pettinicchio 2021). A 2005 UCLA study of Screen Actors Guild members found that only 2 percent of characters on TV identified as having a disability. Another study (Raynor and Hayward 2009) found that only 1 percent of SAG members identify as having a disability.

The 1990s seemed hopeful. There was growing interest by Hollywood to become more inclusive. For example, the hit TV show Will and Grace was celebrated for including gay characters on a network primetime show. But the star of the show, Eric McCormack does not identify as LGBTQ. It prompted scholars like Guillermo Avila-Saavedra (2009) to conclude that there's "Nothing queer about queer television." While McCormack has said that the show did a lot to "educate" Americans on issues like gay marriage, he could not see himself cast in such a role today.[67]

A decade later, the TV show Glee was heralded as ground-breaking for its message of inclusion and equality because it included LGBTQ characters and a character with a disability. Kevin McHale, the actor who played a person with a disability in Glee is not in fact a disabled person. Like McCormack, he told reporters in 2022 that he would not reprise his role as a disabled character in a possible reboot of the show: "If 'Glee' is ever rebooted, Kevin McHale is not signing up to be canceled."[68] And, for good reason: well before the more recent

---

[67] Eric McCormack 'wouldn't get anywhere near' his role in 'Will & Grace' today, www.gaytimes .co.uk/culture/eric-mccormack-says-he-wouldnt-get-anywhere-near-his-will-grace-role-today/.

[68] 'Glee' alum Kevin McHale says he wouldn't play a character in a wheelchair now, *Los Angeles Times*, November 16, 2022.

attention to Whitewashing, disability activists had been fighting against non-disabled actors playing disabled characters.

As Castaneda of the Media Access Office reported, "When a person with a disability sees a positive image on TV that looks like them, their whole attitude changes. It gives them hope for what they can do in the future."[69] The problem is that doing diversity, equity, and inclusion has generally meant a form of "naïve integration" of disability into mainstream culture (Garland-Thomson 2002). In a 2009 post on disabledfeminists.com, author "Anna" not only commented on the recently aired Glee episode prominently featuring McHale, but the positive reception it received from media and the public. Responding to an Associated Press article praising the "wheelchair episode," Anna writes "Thanks, Nice Able-Bodied Lady! I will take your words to heart and just ignore what those silly people with disabilities are saying! It will be better that way!" Anna's comments raised questions about whether these inclusion efforts were just meant to make people without disabilities feel better.

The third disability protest wave therefore coincided with a changing media landscape and greater attention to minority representation. There were both new opportunities for activists to make inroads in this issue area, but also several negative episodes that triggered reactive mobilization by disability activists who used those examples to showcase that their work was nowhere near done.

The year Glee debuted in 2009, the Alliance for Inclusion in the Arts, National Association of the Deaf, and Deaf West Theatre protested a non-Deaf actor playing a Deaf character in the play, "The Heart is a Lonely Hunter." While the play debuted four years earlier in Atlanta and generated no public criticism, activists were now demanding that a Deaf actor be cast in the role. Linda Bove, a Deaf actress and member of the Alliance said: "A hearing actor playing a deaf character is tantamount to putting a white actor in blackface."[70] The theater workshop met with several Deaf actors and searched for some common ground but could not agree on the central issue: Director Doug Hughes said he would not fire the actor who had played Singer in an earlier production of the play in Atlanta. Apparently, Hughes had auditioned Deaf actors for the role in Atlanta but none spoke "well enough to play the part . . ." There was a general sense of confusion and surprise among those in the theater workshop that this was at all controversial or offensive. It was this general unawareness that activists sought to correct through visible protest.

---

[69] www.amsvans.com/blog/glee-wheelchair-actor-kevin-mchale-angers-disability-advocates.
[70] Hearing Man in Deaf Role Stirs Protests in New York, *New York Times*, October 14, 2009.

Responses to activist protests from Hollywood content creators reveal a more generalized attitude among those in positions of power justifying whether some statuses should be represented, and how they should be included. Glee producers basically argued that they picked who they thought was best for the role, even though they "brought in anyone: white, black, Asian, in a wheelchair . . . It was very hard to find people who could really sing, really act, and have that charisma you need on TV."[71] Others point to widespread beliefs among those in charge that hiring disabled people is simply too costly. For example, actor Robert David Hall of the show CSI who walks on two artificial legs, thinks that "there's a fear of litigation, that a person with disabilities might slow a production down, fear that viewers might be uncomfortable."[72] These are similar arguments made by employers that people with disabilities create awkwardness for other employees, and that the cost of hiring a worker with disabilities outweighs any benefit (Maroto and Pettinicchio 2014). These attitudes limit access to the labor market for people with disabilities.

Activist efforts in this issue area point to positive change but they also show how challenging it is to counteract widespread negative beliefs. Protests went a long way not only in raising awareness about representation but also in re-centering the conversation around what should be considered appropriate or meaningful representation. Activists and SMOs found new opportunities to make salient these long-standing grievances, later finding allies in #MeToo to challenge sexist, racist, and ableist practices in Hollywood. Disability activists would also turn inward, challenging their own organizations and networks to do better when it came to inclusion and empowerment.

3.1 From Jerry's Orphans to End the "R Word" Campaign

By the third disability protest wave, issue dynamics had changed. Media and culture related protest came to represent a greater share of protest activity. Although the number of visible protests targeting media and negative portrayals of disability reflect less than a third of protests during the third wave, they were pivotal in garnering a lot of public and media attention, especially online. Protests against the Muscular Dystrophy Association's (MDA) Jerry Lewis Telethon captured early efforts to end pitiable representations of disability and exploiting those depictions to raise money (Shapiro 1993). As early as 1981, activists were already on high alert about the hurtful messages the telethon was broadcasting. June Fine of the group Boston Self-Help told the Boston Globe that the telethon

---

[71] www.usmagazine.com/entertainment/news/disabled-advocates-protest-glees-wheelchair-epi sode-20091111/.

[72] 'Glee' episode irks advocates for disabled, *The Hollywood Reporter*, November 10, 2009.

could at least include more adults with muscular dystrophy, "That way, the public would see that handicapped people are self-sufficient." An MDA spokesperson disagreed with activist criticisms: "We try to depict handicapped people positively. They are not 100 percent useless, and we don't depict them as such."[73] To activists, these responses were insensitive and showed how some long-time disability service-provision groups, MDA among others, were in denial about their messaging.

Longmore's (2015) account of telethons described these American inventions as orchestrated by "charity professionals." He emphasized that telethons were not just about economic and political opportunities, they "shaped popular perceptions" of disability (p. xiv). Throughout the early-to-mid-1990s, activists, many affiliated with the group Jerry's Orphans/Jerry's Protesters, regularly held demonstrations in different cities usually Labor Day weekend when the MDA Telethon hosted by Lewis was held. They were some of the earliest well-publicized examples of visible protests challenging negative portrayals of disability. In 1991, Kris Matthews and Mike Ervin, two former 1960s MDA poster children, began a boycott against the telethon, targeting the telethon's corporate sponsors. Dozens of people protested at a Los Angeles TV station with a simultaneous protest in Las Vegas and Chicago. Protesters held banners reading "Jerry's telethon, annual ritual of shame," and "Jerry maligns the disabled." In a statement, Matthews said "Jerry Lewis keeps perpetuating all those myths and stereotypes about people with disabilities, particularly people with neuromuscular diseases. He uses language like 'cripple' and 'half a person.'"[74]

The following year, Jerry's Orphans protested in Oakland "saying the sentimental extravaganza makes them look pitiful and childlike."[75] In 1993, DIA joined Jerry's Orphans in organizing protests. MDA's Chris Rosa who himself has muscular dystrophy said the organization was doing nothing wrong and that most of the money raised went to patient programs and research. The organization continued to deny they were perpetuating harmful stereotypes about disability. Again, at a 1995 demonstration, twenty-five activists blocked entrances to CBS Television City. They wanted to get their message out to celebrities who participated in the telethon – that it was a "charity racket, schmaltzy, and pity-on-parade."[76] Protesters were doubly outraged that telethon organizers were parking in blue spaces reserved for disabled people.

---

[73] Advocate for handicapped raps Jerry Lewis "telethon," *Boston Globe*, September 5, 1981.
[74] www.upi.com/Archives/1991/09/02/Jerry-Lewis-telethon-hit-by-protests/2331683784000/.
[75] Jerry Lewis Telethon Protested in Oakland, *San Francisco Chronicle*, September 7, 1992.
[76] Protesters Crash Barriers at Jerry Lewis Benefit Telethon, *Los Angeles Times*, September 5, 1995.

By the mid-1990s, groups like DIA and Jerry's Orphans had made their position clear: end the telethon. The MDA continued to claim it was portraying disabled people in a positive light, and there were those who preferred a reform to the telethon rather than ending it entirely.[77] The telethon would still go on for years until 2014. Yet, the telethon protests were important for the disability movement as they carved a path for more systematic challenges against pervasive biases and beliefs deeply embedded in culture. Disability activists continue to challenge negative imagery, taken-for-granted harmful tropes and language, and inauthentic representations of disability. Throughout the third protest wave, most of these efforts were episodic, precipitated by specific events and actions. Organizations and activist networks, though, were ready to act.

The mid-2000s saw several visible protests around the r-word which was still widely used in mainstream films (in fact, several newspaper articles included in the dataset on which my analyses are based use the r-word in their headlines). In 2008, groups like Special Olympics and the American Association of People with Disabilities (AAPD) protested the movie theater premiering Ben Stiller's Tropic Thunder which repeatedly uses the r-word. In addition to the LA protest, groups and activists called for a nationwide boycott of the movie. Quickly, a coalition of groups including NARC, National Down Syndrome Congress, and AAPD took mass action against the film. After screening the movie, the executive director of National Down Syndrome Congress said he "felt personally assaulted." The executive director of NARC told the *New York Times* reporter that he could not recall a mass campaign by disability groups against a movie like this one, although he did note some objections made against the 2004 film Napoleon Dynamite. Surely, part of the motivation for visible protest was driven by how blatant, unabashedly, and unapologetically the r-word was used.

Timothy Shriver of Special Olympics was especially outraged that no one in production raised issues with the repeated use of the word. In fact, original promotional posters included the line "Once upon a time there was a retard" which was later removed when some disability groups rallied against it.[78] He pointed to how producers showed more care and sensitivity around race when the Robert Downey Jr. character (a White soldier) is effectively appearing in blackface. But activists had now grown accustomed to dismissive replies by cultural producers and elites. The response from the studio was that the movie is meant to be satirical and over the top. They would not be editing out the r-word from the movie. They did say they would work with disability groups in the future. The movie brought in 195 million and currently has a 7/10 rating on

---

[77] In Wheelchairs and on Crutches, Some Disabled Protest a Telethon, *New York Times*, September 7, 1993.

[78] Nationwide 'Thunder' Boycott in the Works, *New York Times*, August 11, 2008.

IMDB and 82 percent rating on Rotten Tomatoes. It can still be viewed unedited on streaming services.

That same year, a contestant of reality show, Big Brother, Adam Jasinski, who worked for United Autism Foundation was recorded saying that if he won the reality show, he would use the money to open a hair salon for disabled people "so retards can get it together and get their hair done." Despite its efforts, another group, Autism United, could neither get a formal apology nor a meeting with CBS who aired the show. CBS believed that because another contestant challenged Adam's use of the term, it was allowed to remain in the show. CBS seemed to think they were doing a good thing, treating the incident as a teachable moment. Although Jasinski was fired by the United Autism Foundation, CBS did not alert the cast member as he was sequestered during production of the show.[79] Activists then turned to the show's sponsors. The case received considerable media attention and Autism United was successful in getting sponsors like Lowe's to pull their ads. This also became loosely connected to the "Spread the Word to end the Word" (referring to the r-word) campaign which began a year earlier in 2007.

These examples represent protest's successes as well as ongoing challenges. In 2010, Obama signed a law that would remove the word "mental retardation" from programs and policies. And the r-word is rarely if ever used in contemporary mainstream films or television. Still, nearly a decade later in 2017, students involved with a NARC-run program mobilized to end the use of the r-word. They too were part of the now almost 10-year old "Spread the Word" campaign. One person involved with the program said, "Language affects attitudes and attitudes affect action." They protested at San Francisco City Hall although the protest was not specifically directed at local government. They sought to raise awareness and get people to pledge never to use the word. Protesters said there are alternatives to the r-word: rambunctious, resourceful, resplendent, radiant, and respect.[80]

3.2 Not about Us without Us

The Jerry Lewis Telethon protests had wider meaning for the disability movement. The focus of visible protest was not just on the images and negative portrayals of the telethon itself, but that groups in the disability nonprofit sector used or supported this fundraising strategy. It was emblematic of a broader tension among disability groups on inclusion, control, and decision-making,

---

[79] 'BB' Angers Autistic Group, *New York Post*, February 19, 2008.
[80] San Francisco students push to end use of the r-word, *SFGate*, March 1, 2017.

and which groups empowered disabled people, and which promoted harmful depictions and stereotypes.

As early as the 1970s, many groups purportedly representing disabled people's interests came under fire for being run by non-disabled people, engaging in questionable practices, and perpetuating stereotypes about disability (e.g., Goodwill's reliance on sheltered workshops suggesting people with disabilities cannot be integrated into competitive labor, Friedman 2019; Maroto and Pettinicchio 2022). In short, as former Office of Civil Rights director Martin Gerry said, groups like Goodwill and Easter Seals were increasingly seen as derelicts (Scotch 2001). They were effectively charity groups that were out of touch with the civil rights and minority rights focus of the nascent disability rights movement. Easter Seals and March of Dimes were groups that in the 1950s and 1960s used pity-driven charity campaigns to raise money. In one 1965 campaign, Easter Seals used a photograph of a boy in crutches with the text: "Lend me a dollar to help me walk and I'll make you feel good all Day. P.S. I'll pay you back when I'm rich" (Pettinicchio 2019).

It was in this vein that protesters in the 1990s criticized the MDA – that it is "making millions of dollars and they haven't found anything in all their years of research." Gary Clifra of the Alliance for Research Accountability called the MDA an "institution that just basically processes money and offers false hope."[81] Activists were critical, as they had been with groups like Easter Seals years ago, about the focus on cure and normalization; on changing people with disabilities rather than changing social norms.

Activists increasingly questioned whose interests established disability groups represented, and where voices of people with disabilities were among them. Visible protests played an important part in challenging groups by bringing internal struggles and discontent to light, airing what positions different groups and activists took on issues, and how institutions understood inclusion and representation. The disability cause field was changing from within.

A well-known example involved the appointment of a non-Deaf President, Elisabeth Zinser, to Gallaudet University in 1988 (see Christiansen and Barnartt's account in *Deaf President Now)*. Protesters organized by DUCK, a more radical branch of the National Association of the Deaf, were victorious. I. King Jordan instead became the first Deaf president of the university. The university also planned on adding more Deaf trustees to eventually make the board majority Deaf.[82]

---

[81] www.upi.com/Archives/1991/09/02/Jerry-Lewis-telethon-hit-by-protests/2331683784000/.

[82] Deaf Students Shut College, Demanding Deaf President, *Los Angeles Times*, March 8, 1988.

That same year, a group of disability activists led by Jane Small who had also been involved in then LA Council member Tom Bradley's mayoral campaigns came to protest Bradley's appointment of a non-disabled psychologist to run the Office for the Disabled. As a reporter for the LA Times wrote, "To some disabled people, the hiring was as surprising as if Bradley named a man to run the city Commissions on the Status of Women or designated a white aide as his liaison to black neighborhoods in South-Central Los Angeles."[83] One protester said, "We the disabled people of Los Angeles just want to speak for ourselves." The mayor's office cast those resigning from council in protest as an ungrateful few who should credit Bradley for creating the office in the first place.

A few years later, blind people protested the charity Lighthouse for not having blind people on its board of directors. As one protester said, "The Lighthouse is a failure and has always been a failure because you are not in touch with blind people."[84] Groups like the National Federation of the Blind continue to keep vigil over representation among service-provision organizations. And organizations have made important changes to how they are governed. A 2019 Braille Monitor article written by Lighthouse's president, Bryan Bashin, says much about the organization's current structure and identity: "Led by the Blind: Bringing Authenticity to Services for the Blind and Making Them Relevant to the Lives We Want to Live."[85]

Autism is another important area peppered with visible protest events which showcase struggles not only with challenging broader social norms around disability, but also challenging other groups within the immediate field. For years, the National Society for Autistic Children founded in 1965 and later renamed Autism Society of America dominated the advocacy and service-provision field. Forty years later, the proliferation of autism-related groups brought new perspectives sometimes on long-time grievances, and other times, new issues more prominent in the third disability protest wave including misperceptions and negative images. Over the last decade, organizations in the disability cause field increasingly heeded the movement rallying cry "not about us without us" in challenging what they see as organizations *for* the disabled but not *by* people with disabilities.

For example, like Autism United, Autism Self-Advocacy Network (ASAN) also founded in 2006 was organized by and for people with Autism. In 2008, Autism United organized a protest of over fifty people against Michael Savage's radio show, "The Savage Nation" for "spiteful and harmfully misleading

---

[83] Group of Disabled Assail Bradley; 6 Quit as Advisers, *Los Angeles Times*, April 22, 1988.
[84] Blind People Protest To Lighthouse Board, *San Francisco Chronicle*, April 26, 1990.
[85] https://nfb.org/images/nfb/publications/fr/fr38/4/fr380413.htm.

comments about autistic children as a result of bad parenting."[86] In 2010, the organization made headlines when its founder, Ari Ne'eman, was nominated by President Obama to Autism Speaks – a nonprofit autism awareness organization. He would be its first nominee to have autism.

Ironically, Ne'eman and his organization had protested Autism Speaks just a year prior over their fundraising video. Autism Speaks had merged with Cure Autism Now, founded by Jonathan Shestack who openly criticized Ne'eman's 2010 nomination. The 2009 fundraising campaign used Shestack's "kidnapped" analogy: "If 1 in 150 American children were kidnapped, we'd have a national emergency. We do. Autism." Ne'eman told the York Daily Record[87] that:

> Advocacy groups need to learn from the physical disability community, which stopped using scare tactics because they only widened the understanding gap between those with disabilities and those who don't have them, which in turn actually increased discrimination.

Shestack stood by the slogan while Susan Wallace of Autism Speaks diplomatically proclaimed "Groups of people who mean well get into arguments, and autism advocacy suffers. Until different organizations can unite that won't change."

These divisions would however deepen. A year later, Lee Grossman of Autism Society of America noted the split in the autism advocacy community: either one accepts neurodiversity as part of one's identity, or they search for a cure and genetic screening. Autism Speaks still used language like "struggling with autism" and focused on awareness rather than acceptance. ASAN continued to challenge Autism Speaks' yearly campaigns as sending the wrong message, like for example, 2015's "Light It Up Blue."[88]

In 2017, the ASAN condemned World Autism Awareness Day and White House participation in Autism Speaks' Light It Up Blue. President Trump proclaimed his administration will encourage "innovation that will lead to new treatments and cures for autism." In response, ASAN's news brief stated that the "Trump administration's attempt to revive the idea of cure is a dangerous fringe position." ASAN also sought to connect their grievances to the broader issue of homecare which regained salience because of threats of retrenchment and the involvement of Resistors in challenging ACA repeal efforts. ASAN argued that Autism Speaks had aligned themselves with a government that has sought to repeal ACA and Medicaid.[89]

---

[86] Some call for firing of radio talk show host, *Boston Herald*, July 22, 2008.

[87] Critics topple billboard Autism York said it did not intend to offend anybody with the sign, *York Daily Record*, August 28, 2009.

[88] Speaking Out against Autism Speaks, Even If It Means No Ice Cream, *New York Times*, June 4, 2015.

[89] ASAN Condemns White House Autism Proclamation, *Targeted News Service*, April 1, 2017.

ASAN acknowledged that progress in fighting negative images of autism had been made over the last ten years but more needed to be done. In 2019, the group condemned Sesame Street's ties to Autism Speaks. The children's educational program consulted with Autism Speaks on the Muppet who has autism. ASAN contends that Autism Speaks encourages parents "to view autism as a terrible disease from which their child can 'get better.'"[90]

When it came to raising awareness and challenging taken-for-granted stereotypes perpetuated by media and other cultural sites and beyond, disability organizations and especially, visible protests, were successful over the long-term. Attitudes are often evasive and difficult to challenge in the abstract, but activists learned how to focus and channel their grievances toward specific targets – from telethons to TV and radio shows, to other nonprofit and service-provision groups. It is true that visible protests alone did not end telethons. TV stations began dropping them as they had more competition in overnight hours and started charging charities to air them (Longmore 2015). And while the r-word is rarely if ever used in mainstream content, the r-word is still used a great deal in social media.[91] Nevertheless, these protests started a public conversation continuing to keep the issue current and in the spotlight.

4 The Outcomes of Visible Protest

Visible protest waves involve activists and groups mobilizing resources in response to a mix of opportunity and threat activating grievances across interconnected issue areas aimed at multiple targets. Political opportunities and resources may be shared across issue areas not only because issue areas and corresponding grievances are intertwined, but also because the same organizations engaged in one issue area are also engaged in others (e.g., DIA, AAPD, and PVA were involved in everything from transit to health protests, to Jerry's Orphans). Groups and networks drew from the same tactical repertoires in considering their goals, activities, and targets across issue areas. Yet, outcomes of visible protest vary considerably across waves and issue areas.

Protest outcomes are often difficult to define. It requires analyzing issue developments and movement goals before and after protest events which can mean a wide time interval around that given protest event. Outcomes can result in both short- and long-term gains. Additionally, activist beliefs about success and failure may not always coincide with more "objective" appraisals of social movement outcomes. Analyses of protest outcomes must consider the more

---

[90] How a 'Sesame Street' Muppet became embroiled in a controversy over autism, *Washington Post*, September 19, 2019.

[91] www.specialolympics.org/discriminatory-language-about-people-with-intellectual-disabilities-particularly-the-r-word-remains-prevalent-across-social-media.

subjective understandings of success and failure. This is important because how activists view the outcomes of protest dictates how they move forward.

Before the 1970s, people with disabilities were not thought able to represent their own interests as a political constituency, let alone organize disruptive visible protests. Afterall, activists had no guarantee that early protests would lead to any gains.[92] That all changed when first-wave protests became seen as viable, legitimate, and successful tools in effecting policy change, and in changing meanings around disability.

Early discrimination-based protests were certainly treated by activists and leaders as having achieved their goals. And, as Table 3 shows, discrimination protests had some of the highest success rates. Judy Heumann recently described those first wave protests in her 2018 Ted Talk:

> In 1972, President Nixon vetoed the Rehabilitation Act. We protested. He signed it. Then the regulations that needed to be promulgated to implement that law had not in fact been signed. We demonstrated. They were signed. And when the Americans With Disabilities Act, the ADA, our Emancipation Proclamation Act, looked as though it might not in fact be passed in the House or Senate, disabled people from all across the United States came together and they crawled up the Capitol steps. That was an amazing day, and the House and Senate passed the ADA. And then President Bush signed the ADA.

Disruptive visible disability protests had become part of American political culture. First-wave protests generated a sense of collective efficacy, agency, and control (Corcoran, Pettinicchio, and Young 2011; Pfaff 2006). As Table 3 shows, discrimination-related visible protests which were a large part of the first protest wave saw some form of success 54 percent of the time. Along with employment-related protests, discrimination-based protests were the most successful (on average across issue areas the full success rate is closer to 30 percent).

What made discrimination protests successful? One reason might be organizational: disability organizations were present in 83 percent of all discrimination protest events. This is higher than average, which is about 50 percent.[93] But, overall, the presence of disability organizations did not increase the chances of success by all that much. Just over 53 percent of protests leading to successful outcomes were associated with a disability group. Organizational presence alone may not be enough to explain outcomes.

---

[92] Militant Advocacy Group for Disabled Revels in Role as Agitator, *New York Times*, October 10, 1991.

[93] The average number of groups to event in the disability rights movement is lower than other constituencies, with usually a single organization coordinating a given protest. Soule and Earl (2005) found that in 1960, the average number of groups at a protest across many different movements was slightly fewer than 2 and reached a high of 2.5 in the early 1970s, declining to about 1.5 in the 1980s.

Table 3 Outcomes of visible protest by issue area

Issue Area	Employment	Transportation	Healthcare	Education	Social Welfare	Discrimination	Media Cultural Sites
Outcomes							
Not Achieved	16.7	52.3	46.0	60.9	58.6	16.7	50.0
Partially Achieved	33.3	29.5	33.3	26.1	22.4	29.2	25.0
Achieved	50.0	18.2	20.6	13.0	19.0	54.2	25.0
	100.0	100.0	100.0	100.0	100.0	100.0	100.0

Table 4 Outcomes of visible protest by goal type

	Goal			
	More/Better Services	Expand/ Protect Rights	Increase Spending/ Stop Cuts	Raise Awareness about Portraying Disability
Outcomes				
Not Achieved	44.4	38.7	58.9	36.0
Partially Achieved	40.7	29.3	22.4	36.0
Achieved	14.8	32.0	18.7	28.0
	100	100	100	100

Table 5 Outcomes of visible protest by target

	Target			
	Federal Government	State Government	Local Government	Businesses/ Organizations
Outcomes				
Not Achieved	33.8	58.8	57.4	50.0
Partially Achieved	29.9	25.5	24.1	32.7
Achieved	36.4	15.7	18.5	17.3
	100	100	100	100

Perhaps it has more to do with a combination of protest goals and political opportunities and how groups helped to identify and define both (Gamson 1975). In general, the goal of expanding/protecting rights saw the highest success rates (see Table 4). Antidiscrimination protests in the first wave focused on mobilizing rights-based legislation at a time when rights were expanding to include multiple marginalized groups.

How activists and groups adapt to shifting issue politics and their protracted interaction with elite targets through the regular political process can also shape outcomes (Goldstone 1980), especially in the long term. With discrimination, the federal government made up 71 percent of protest targets. Conversely, in the social welfare issue area, the federal government only makes up 33 percent of targets. The success of discrimination protests is partly related to the targets of those protests. As Table 5 shows, visible protests targeting the federal government overall see better odds of achieving or partially achieving their objectives while visible protests targeting state governments are among the least successful (see Table 5).

Table 6 provides further empirical insight into these potential explanations. In addition to strong evidence that protests have been most successful in the

Table 6 Logit models predicting outcomes of visible protest

	Model 1	Model 2	Model 3	Model 4	Model 5
Issue Area (Referent: Discrimination)					
Employment	1.000	0.986	1.130	1.500	1.100
	(1.230)	(1.160)	(1.340)	(2.010)	(1.503)
Transportation	0.183**	0.250*	0.334	0.350	0.249
	(0.114)	(0.166)	(0.229)	(0.238)	(0.187)
Healthcare	0.234*	0.283*	0.374	0.373	0.285
	(0.142)	(0.172)	(0.267)	(0.264)	(0.219)
Education	0.129**	0.160*	0.177*	0.209*	0.145*
	(0.09)	(0.117)	(0.141)	(0.166)	(0.123)
Social Welfare	0.141**	0.186**	0.245	0.264	0.181*
	(0.086)	(0.117)	(0.184)	(0.193)	(0.143)
Media/Cultural Sites	0.200**	0.254	0.141	0.211	0.156
	(0.150)	(0.198)	(0.145)	(0.21)	(0.169)
Target (Referent: Federal Government)					
State		0.410*	0.427*	0.351*	0.379*
		(0.163)	(0.175)	(0.151)	(0.166)
Local		0.510	0.485	0.444	0.482
		(0.210)	(0.207)	(0.204)	(0.219)
Businesses/Organizations		0.575	0.377*	0.300*	0.318*
		(0.246)	(0.174)	(0.150)	(0.160)

Table 6 (cont.)

	Model 1	Model 2	Model 3	Model 4	Model 5
Goal Type (Ref: More/Better Services)					
Expand/Protect Rights			0.816	0.935	0.964
			(0.501)	(0.574)	(0.600)
Increase/Stop Spending Cuts			0.489	0.573	0.578
			(0.237)	(0.281)	(0.289)
Raise Awareness/Portrayals			2.530	3.793	4.219
			(1.862)	(2.960)	(3.457)
Other Joint Activities (Referent: None)					
Work with Elites				4.000**	4.272**
				(1.894)	(2.100)
Testifying/Lobbying				2.089*	2.151*
				(0.762)	(0.803)
Litigation				5.408**	5.464**
				(2.709)	(2.747)
Other				3.559	3.940
				(3.255)	(3.879)
Disability Organizations					0.687
					(0.252)
Other Organizations					0.704
					(0.240)

Constant	5.000	6.440	8.050	3.615	6.500
	(2.740)	(3.590)	(6.760)	(3.072)	(6.165)
Wald Chi–2	13.98	20.000*	25.990**	38.250***	40.840**
Pseudo R2	0.0543	0.070	0.093	0.150	0.150

Odds ratios. Robust standard errors in parentheses. *$p < 0.05$, **$p < 0.01$, ***$p < 0.001$. $N = 234$ visible protest events. Dependent variable 1 = success/partial success, 0 = failure.

discrimination issue area (all other issue areas have a decreased likelihood of success in comparison), failure rates are higher when targeting local and state governments compared to the federal government. Organizational presence, as expected given the nearly 50/50 split among all protest events, does not significantly increase the odds of success. In terms of goals, I use "more or better services" as a referent because this goal type has the highest failure rate. While raising awareness is the only goal type which comparatively increases success rates, the variable is not significant.

I drew from discrimination and the civil rights area because protest in this area experienced the highest success. Not all discrimination-based protests were successful. Looking at why protests were not successful in an issue area with the highest success rates might shed light on failure across issue areas more generally.

Problems around equal access continued well after the first wave of protest. Despite having moved the rights agenda further, the future of equal rights remained uncertain in large part because of negative attitudes and relatedly, compliance problems. Even after new ADA compliance rules, the Service Employees International Union in August 1993, investigated nearly fifty businesses, offices, and organizations in DC. They found "serious, and obvious barriers to people with disabilities."[94] Although federal legislation prompted these protests, the federal government had already become less relevant as a target of protest for the disability movement. Rather, twenty demonstrators placed "Unwelcome Mats" in front of doorways, including that of the US Chamber of Commerce. The Chamber's response: use the back entrance.

Even with a well-established organizational base and resources, activists were not successful in the short-term in getting these businesses to accommodate, pointing to how long it may take for change to come about and how uneven that change is. Protesters were especially irked by the Chamber's failure to comply because it was "sending a terrible message that people with disabilities have back-door and second-class access."

Protesters took to the streets again a few months later chanting "No Access, No Peace." If they were not going to get businesses to comply, they would at least "embarrass the owners"[95] as one protester said. Although the Service Employees International Union also filed a complaint with the Justice Department and testified regularly in Congress about persistent accessibility problems, the response from businesses were mixed. The business community continued to think activist grievances were either absurd or unimportant.

---

[94] Protesters Want Wheelchair Ramp at US Chamber, *Washington Post*, August 18, 1993.

[95] Barriers to Disabled Protested at NW Building: Structure Violates New Law, Group Says, *Washington Post*, October 1, 1993.

This would only fuel more visible protests during the third wave, and a growing focus on the ways in which various public settings still discriminated against people with disabilities. For example, activists were unable to include provisions in the Help America Vote Act which would have guaranteed that states make voting places and machines accessible to people with disabilities.[96] Then in 2009, disability activists took on Disney Parks. Protests organized by the National Association of the Deaf and Deaf West Theater rejected a settlement regarding Disney's ban of Segways – self-balancing transportation machines. The DOJ began drafting regulations to address whether everything from Disney to malls could ban the use of Segways and other devices for people with disabilities.[97] It would be an ongoing issue leading to several lawsuits. Finally, the Court of Appeals in 2013 sided with Disney that it can ban Segways. Disney did, however, develop its own version of a Segway. Changing attitudes proved to be challenging even with disability rights legislation long in place, illustrating the kinds of partial solutions that keep issues open and grievances only temporarily submerged.

These examples also illustrate the coevolution of issue politics and mobilization. Over time, discrimination-based protest increasingly moved from proactive measures to ensure the expansion of rights to reaction around implementation problems and elite efforts to backtrack on policy commitments. During the first disability protest wave, extending rights did not immediately invoke budgetary concerns or questions about cost. Cost and inefficiencies of cost and efficiency would later become a key part of the rationale among political elites to limit rights and antidiscrimination policies. For example, the case against unfunded mandates further pit rights against the alleged costs of implementation, making rights a platitude weak in practice.

On the other hand, about 72 percent of social welfare–related visible protests were related to social spending. These were most often reactionary across all three protest waves as they sought to prevent what were typically inevitable program cuts as part of broader austerity measures exogenous to the disability cause field. Although constituents fought back, the kinds of cuts being made specifically affecting people with disabilities may not have been seen as politically important compared to say, those directly affecting senior citizens, for example (Campbell 2003; Pierson 1994). When push came to shove, policymakers may have been choosing programs to axe that they believed were least politically costly. Social welfare visible protests also relied on local networks and less so on formal organizations. State governments represent 47 percent of

---

[96] Disabled Protesters Block Doors at End of Meeting on Elections, *New York Times*, May 19, 2004.

[97] A Two-Wheeled Protest at Federal Court, *New York Times*, June 4, 2009.

social welfare visible protest targets which see much less success compared to those targeting the federal government (see Table 5). Even within healthcare, where protests overall led to significantly more partial victories (see Table 3), almost half of visible protests sought to increase spending to healthcare or, to prevent spending cuts; cuts which were ultimately implemented.

People with disabilities were certainly a big part of the collective efforts saving ACA which had implications for homecare. As cofounder of Indivisible, Ezra Levin, explained:

> One of the striking things about the past several months was the breadth and depth of coordinated action across the progressive ecosystem. Indivisible groups cheered on or linked arms with activists from National ADAPT, Planned Parenthood, MoveOn, Ultraviolet, Center for Popular Democracy and Credo Mobile, among others. The common feature of these organiza- tions' work over the past several months was simple: constituent power, relentlessly applied.

Yet, success may also have been mitigated by some loftier goals of the disability movement which in many cases, required an overhaul of Social Security. The fight for homecare continues with little by way of structural reforms necessary to fully address de-institutionalization, an issue albeit made more salient during the COVID-19 pandemic.[98] ACA did not solve this problem. Healthcare pro- tests illustrate a mix of short and long-term goals and outcomes. Even when political opportunities presented themselves and powerful civil rights frames used, they were not enough for either activists or sympathetic policy elites to overcome the hurdles associated with major structural reforms.

Another important dimension capturing the relationship between activists and elites may have more to do with tactics. About 63 percent of all visible protest events were linked to the use of less visible, more institutional tactics. Among visible protests tied to institutional tactics, 20 percent involved working with elites and decision makers, 20 percent court cases, and a whopping 57 percent participating in hearings or lobbying policymakers. The latter activity is highly associated with targeting the federal government, and to a lesser extent state governments. Litigation represented over a third of the other activities across state and local governments, as well as those targeting businesses and organizations.

Discrimination-related visible protests were the most likely to also be asso- ciated with testifying or lobbying (mostly Congress). This makes sense given the role played by political entrepreneurs in Congress in setting the disability rights agenda. They reflected political opportunities and routine access to elites,

---

[98] Why won't Ohio boost pay for home care workers?, *Daily Record*, December 5, 2021; For vulnerable, long wait for home care help drags on, *Star Tribune*, August 22, 2022

like for example, the Senate Subcommittee on the Handicapped which regularly invited movement leaders to hearings. In the education issue area, protest success is among the lowest and this may be because education has the fewest visible protest events associated with other more institutional movement tactics.

As Table 6 shows, visible protests which were also simultaneously associated with lobbying, litigation, and working with elites had a significantly higher success rate. The disability movement provides a good example of how, over a protracted period, groups used both institutional and extra-institutional tactics at the same time. In that way, organizations, when linked to tactics and goals, may have a possible indirect effect in shaping protest outcomes as they help devise strategy and identify opportunities for action. For example, 90 percent of healthcare-related visible protests where lobbying was also involved were directly tied to disability organizations. ADAPT was considered among the most disruptive of groups but it too engaged in lobbying, litigation, and worked with elites at all levels of government. It had a variety of objectives: from total transit accessibility to a complete overhaul of Medicaid, to meetings with local authorities and raising public awareness. Established, professional hybrid service-advocacy groups like PVA, Disabled American Veterans, and National Paraplegia Foundation were also involved in both disruptive protests as well as routine lobbying activity.

Groups oscillated between seeking to displace the establishment and challenge an elite-based status quo, while working with elites to bring change about incrementally. And while protest goals may begin as lofty, they adapt to the political context, and success is in part determined by ongoing adaptation. For example, in 1989, the Golden Gate Regional Center demanded that Republican members of the assembly pass the California State budget. Ultimately, mental health and disability laws were not adequately implemented due to budgetary concerns. They could also not stop program cuts, but they did get government officials to create a commission to investigate policy implementation and included community leaders in that process. This shows the multipronged approach movements take to effect change (Pettinicchio 2012) as well as flexibility among organizations (Staggenborg 2020) where groups have other ways of shaping change other than through visible protests.

An important reason demanding this multipronged approach is that issue politics are in flux and involve multiple targets, goals, and well-rounded strategies. For example, affordable and accessible housing is an issue at all three levels of government. In July 2008, Congress mandated that Freddie and Fannie contribute 0.04 percent of new mortgage purchases to the National Housing Trust Fund and the Capital Magnet Fund to establish dedicated revenue for low-income housing which many people with disabilities use. The Trust would work with states. However, shortly thereafter, as the government took massive steps to rescue the two firms from collapse, their conservator, the Federal Housing Finance Agency, suspended the payments before any were made. Groups of activists from different communities many brought together by the Right to the City coalition, protested also filing a series of lawsuits on the matter. Housing remains a problem. Recently, in New York in 2021, with the help of the Legal Aid Society, lawyers successfully argued that preexisting conditions put many homeless people at a "higher risk of severe consequences" if they contracted COVID-19. At the same time, about twenty-five homeless people with disabilities along with housing and social welfare activists protested the Department of Homeless Services for forcibly removing over 8000 homeless people currently living in hotels toward "barracks-style shelters" in the city.[99]

Short-term and partial success does not mean that issues and grievances are resolved. On the contrary, disability activism reveals an ongoing struggle in settling issues, in part because of the many veto points and policy cycles that facilitate retrenchment, and the litany of partial solutions offered to quell contention.

The healthcare issue area is a good example of ongoing structural problems where protests faced a relatively high degree of failure, but also some partial victories and partial policy solutions. Activists and groups recognized very early on that changing the system was going to be a long-term goal requiring multiple tactics. In 1991, in an early Medicaid/homecare-related protest that received much media coverage, ADAPT protested then Arkansas governor Clinton's proposed cuts to Medicaid which would have affected community-based care. Their efforts at the state-level coupled with the group's tireless efforts testifying before Congress on homecare led to Clinton restoring the cuts.[100] A year later, ADAPT tied the homecare issue to the recently enacted ADA and received national attention and support by the Gore-Clinton campaign, even though Clinton as president left the issue of homecare to states.[101] As a protester in a 1994 DC homecare demonstration said, "We've got a long way to go to get what we want, and we've got to work on the legislators to get it."[102]

In 2009, the American Lung Association, Health Access California, and the United Long-Term Care Workers Union protested Gov. Arnold Schwarzenegger's sweeping cuts to homecare benefits, education, Medicaid, and HIV services.[103]

[99] N.Y.C.'s Plan to Move Homeless People from Hotel Is Blocked by a Judge, *New York Times*, September 21, 2021.

[100] The Disabled Protest And Clinton Yields, *San Francisco Chronicle*, January 1, 1992.

[101] Protesters in Wheelchairs Block Clinton Headquarters in S.F., *San Francisco Chronicle*, October 20, 1992.

[102] Disabled Meet Clinton, Stage March, *Washington Post*, May 3, 1994.

[103] Seeking a way out of the mess; California is at the mercy of Wall St. for a loan as cash dwindles, *Los Angeles Times*, May 23, 2009.

In addition to massive letter-writing campaigns, the United Long-Term Care Workers Union was also involved in the *Martinez* v. *Schwarzenegger* case. The case was an important success for activists as the court ruled that California violated the Medicaid Act and that cuts would cause irreparable harm for those receiving in-home health services forcing them to turn to institutionalized care.

Visible protests illustrate where activists can make inroads and where they continue to face challenges. They point to how groups and activist networks mobilize resources, turn grievances into action, respond to changes in political opportunities, identify targets, and engage in institutional tactics to supplement more disruptive action. Visible protests also did much to put the disability rights movement on the political map where today, it has become almost taken-for-granted that Americans with disabilities will mobilize on the streets to have their voices heard.

4.1 How Visible Protests Changed the Disability Movement

Protesters may not always have a clear idea about the intended goals of any one event, how those goals may change based on mobilization and issue politics, or what a protest event might mean in the grand scheme of things. As one protester at a 2003 rally held outside the Justice Department put it "We're feeling good that there's a beginning, and we'll have to wait and see what happens from there."[104] For activists, there was a sense that taking direct action was necessary. And even if activist involvement may often have been motivated by very specific grievances like stopping budget cuts, taking down a radio host, or getting working wheelchair lifts on buses, there was also widespread belief that disruptive protests were part of a broader long-term project for the disability movement and for American politics. This long-term project meant finding ways of bringing grievances, goals, and objectives to the broader public, and visible protests played that very important role.

Visible disability protests drew attention to the societal obstacles that marginalize and exclude people with disabilities. It raised awareness and brought issues to bystanders and conscience constituents by disrupting their everyday routines – showcasing the ableist nature of some of the most mundane activities. Transit protests are a good example. In Los Angeles in 1985, when ADAPT protesters blocked Greyhound buses, passengers seemed sympathetic, albeit inconvenienced: "Two passengers appeared surprised and baffled by the protest ... Michael Galloway, 23, said he was sympathetic to the group wanting equal access to buses and waited patiently until the protesters dispersed. 'I see where they are coming from,' Galloway said. 'I hope something is done about

---

[104] Seeking a better Deal for the Disabled Activists Disperse, *Washington Post*, May 13, 2003.

it.'"[105] Even in healthcare-related events, like a 1994 demonstration where around 1,000 protesters carrying signs saying "Real Health Care for All" made their way across the Memorial Bridge in DC, they were applauded by joggers occasionally fist-bumping protesters in support.[106]

Protests generated some empathy and raised awareness. Yet, as activists remind us, the point of visible protest is to disrupt daily routines and challenge norms. People do not like their plans disrupted. In the large multi-rally protests organized by a coalition of students, teachers, people affected by police killings, AIDS-activists, and disabled people in New York in 1995, bystanders stuck in traffic made remarks ranging from "I told my wife to run them over" to "We would have been sympathetic to them. But this is no way to get attention." Similarly, a few years later also in the New York area where several protesters blocked buses without working wheelchair lifts, some passing by yelled "Stop wasting our tax money ... You have plenty of transportation options."[107] These public reactions signaled that more had to be done to change people's hearts and minds, but may also have been a reminder about the possible diminishing returns of protest's "overuse" (Gamson 2004; Ketchley and El-Rayyes 2021). By the second protest wave, activists were ready for short-term backlash, but expected long-term rewards.[108]

Bringing attention to the cause through visible protests sometimes led to arrests, which generally increased attention to the issue. Several factors can affect willingness to arrest protesters, from local political dynamics, to whether the police feel threatened although generally, arrests tend to be relatively uncommon across movements and cause fields (Earl, Soule, and McCarthy 2003; Elliott et al. 2022; Soule and Davenport 2009). Arrests were not too common in disability protests, reported in less than one-fifth of all events. About 60 percent of events leading in arrests were associated with ADAPT which also meant that arrests were more common in transit and healthcare-related protests. Most times, the police let demonstrations end peacefully.

Jokingly, in response to her own question to a Ted Talk audience about how many people it took to block traffic in Manhattan, Heumann said "Fifty. One would be too little. Fifty people. And there were no accessible paddy wagons, so they had to just kind of deal with us." In the *New York Times* article covering the event Heumann is referring to, a police officer was asked about whether they would move the protesters out. He replied, "And where would we get the vehicles, if we did something like that? Besides, traffic isn't being tied up too

---

[105] Disabled People Block Bus at Terminal, *Los Angeles Times*, February 10, 1985.

[106] Disabled Meet Clinton, Stage March, *Washington Post*, May 3, 1994.

[107] A Wheelchair User Can't Get on a Bus, So He Blocks One, *New York Times*, June 27, 2003.

[108] Rush-Hour Protest Causes Gridlock, *New York Times*, April 26, 1995.

much." Police were reluctant to arrest protesters, even when protesters demanded to be arrested. At a 1988 Greyhound demonstration, protesters openly said they were hoping to be arrested but the police captain said they "had no intention of taking these folks into custody" and that "booking a person in a wheelchair is about a 12-hour process each, and we don't intend to arrest them."[109] Similarly, in 2003, at a homecare-related protest, over 100 protesters organized by ADAPT stopped traffic before Justice Department headquarters, and the police let them. The police chief reasoned that past ADAPT protests ended voluntarily and arrests were not needed: "People look for us to do that sort of thing [make arrests], and if we do make arrests, we wind up getting criticized."[110]

Disruption had become necessary, as one activist put it, because using peaceful tactics, while preferable, had already been tried, alluding in part to the long history of disability groups working with elites: "if they don't listen to us, we have to do more."[111] At a 1997 DC homecare protest, Bob Kafta of ADAPT said "We've been waiting too long to get a hearing."[112] The general attitude was that across different issue areas whether healthcare, transit, or social welfare, disabled people were at an institutional impasse. Anthony Trocchia, a wheelchair transit rider who led a demonstration in Queens over inaccessible buses in 2003 put it best when he said: "I got tired of waiting for a bus with a working wheelchair lift, so I decided to try and create a media circus . . . a civil disobedience action." Legislation was simply not doing enough to improve people's daily lives. Responding to the transit authority's position that they had buses to transport him, Trocchia said "This has been going on a long time. It's not just a matter of getting on a bus."[113]

Institutional tactics certainly gave the disability cause legitimacy among policymakers. But visible disability protests made both elites and the public take the efforts of activists more seriously as an organized social movement. As one reporter described, "People with disabilities have become an important, well-coordinated political force in recent years."[114]

A broad spectrum of activists was increasingly making the case that protest was necessary because grievances were not being addressed through regular politics and the injustices they experience are not being taken seriously enough. By the mid-1980s during the second protest wave, as the disability

---

[109] Disabled Group Wants Access on Greyhound, *Los Angeles Times*, August 13, 1988.

[110] Protest Shuts Constitution Ave, *Washington Post*, May 13, 2003.

[111] A Cry for Freedom and an Outcry Over the Killings, *Washington Post*, May 10, 1993.

[112] Disabled Hold Protest on Capitol Hill, *Washington Post*, November 11, 1997.

[113] A Wheelchair User Can't Get on a Bus, So He Blocks One, *New York Times*, June 27, 2003.

[114] Ruling on Disability Rights Called a Blow by Advocates, *New York Times*, February 22, 2001.

organizational field came to include a far greater number of political advocacy groups (Minkoff 1999; Pettinicchio 2019), protest had become a regular part of many organizations' tactical repertoires. Protests however, also aired internal movement schisms because protests not only challenged targets, but they also challenged how things were done within the movement itself.

In his 1980 account of the "wheelchair lobby" in the *Washington Post*, Bud Lemke interviewed Orange County disability activists who believed their political clout in the movement was much weaker than groups and activists who organized large disruptive protests in other American cities. There was concern about identifying with movements on the left[115] and that "push[ing] too hard, they provoke a backlash."[116] His account pointed to concerns about relying on disruption and its potential negative impacts on the cause. There are several examples of growing tensions between activists, leaders, and groups in the disability movement. For example, in the mid-1970s, the well-established and well-entrenched group NARC protested New York State Governor Carey's vetoing of a bill creating a separate office for developmental and intellectual disabilities. It had tremendous support in the legislature. Opponents within the disability community framed the bill as supporting the vested interests of NARC and not individuals who require support who do not have developmental or intellectual disabilities.[117]

These kinds of tensions within a cause field are not uncommon. Movement scholars like Morris (1986) described tensions between established civil rights groups like the NAACP that relied on institutional tactics and their relationships with elites and newer groups like CORE and SNCC coming out of the networks of Black churches who coordinated large-scale disruptive protests. Staggenborg (1986) noted similar tensions among organizations in early pro-choice movement coalitions.

There were growing conflicts specifically around tactics in the disability movement too. Liz Spayed, who covered DC homecare protests wrote that ADAPT's use of "militant tactics has sometimes drawn criticism from other disability rights groups who would prefer to rely on more peaceful means to

---

[115] Disability activists and the disability rights movement have generally been viewed as aligned with the left on many key issues. The disability rights movement was also associated with movements on the left likely because of the tactics they borrowed and adapted from the movements of the 1960s and 1970s. Yet not all issues and groups aligned with so-called left issues. For example, on abortion and assisted dying, some groups like Not Dead Yet aligned with the conservatives and the Christian Right (the Terry Schiavo case, for example). Protests highlight the heterogenous and complicated nature of disability activism. Americans with disabilities are not ideologically monolithic and are often politically evenly divided (www.pewresearch.org/fact-tank/2016/09/22/a-political-profile-of-disabled-americans/).

[116] The Wheelchair Lobby Tries to Get Rolling, *Los Angeles Times*, March 9, 1980.

[117] Bill on retarded is facing a veto, *New York Times*, May 4, 1975.

attain their goals."[118] By the end of the 1980s, ADAPT had become *the* disability protest organization. The *New York Times* article "Militant Advocacy Group for Disabled Revels in Role as Agitator" recounts how ADAPT "exasperated its allies as much as its adversaries." But one ADAPT leader in response said that "I think that even for the people with disabilities who don't participate directly in ADAPT, we give them heart." According to Auberger, ADAPT has a broader purpose – it is a weapon: "we make all the other groups seem real rational."

However, ADAPT activists and leaders also criticized more established groups who they believed had gotten too close to political elites supporting the status quo. In their 1987 newsletter, Incitement Incitement, most headlines showcased the effectiveness of ADAPT's disruptive protest, for example in Phoenix and in the nation's capital. One headline read, "Who's Side is PVA ON? Paralyzed Veterans Declare War Against ADAPT." Founded in 1947, PVA was heavily involved in institutional advocacy but also engaged in visible protests. It had apparently grown concerned with ADAPT's strong reliance on disruptive protests. According to the story, PVA sought to disassociate from ADAPT at a transit protest calling it "illegal civil disobedience." PVA allegedly threatened to end relationships with their members if they participated in ADAPT-led protests. ADAPT's leadership depicted PVA as being "more concerned with their 'professional' image and fundraising prowess than they were with the rights of people with disabilities. But their strongly worded response went far beyond that:

> ADAPT is amazed that the PVA's abhorrence to civil disobedience could cause the PVA to outlaw an organization because the PVA does not embrace the philosophical position that one hundred percent accessibility is more important than our tactics. Therefore; we can only conclude that during the sixties and even today, PVA could not support the Black civil rights movement, Rev. Martin Luther King's, and the Southern Christian Leadership Conferences, because they used Confrontational civil disobedience to publicize the Black man's plight. This obviously left them allied with the KKK and the other oppressors because they did not like the tactics of the Black man. [Incitement Incitement, a Publication of ADAPT, Spring 1987 vol. 3 no 2, p. 4]

Visible protests are important for understanding social and political change as well as issue- movement cycles. Activists saw protests as both symbolic and as an exercise of power over change.[119] Protest turned targets into opponents and

---

[118] A Cry for Freedom and an Outcry Over the Killings, *Washington Post*, May 10, 1993.

[119] Disabled Protesters Achieve A Partial Victory in Atlanta, *Washington Post*, September 27, 1989 and Militant Advocacy Group for Disabled Revels in Role as Agitator, *New York Times*, October 10, 1991.

broadcast the kinds of oppositional frames and justifications that were used to undermine disabled people. Identifying targets was critical for the movement as Auberger said, "You have to have a bad guy in political organizing, somebody you can go after."[120] Protests also helped to identify the key issues in the disability rights struggle, along with problems, and solutions, in the most visible way.

Visible protest changed American politics and the disability movement. Protest became more routinely used and brought the disability movement out from behind a cloak of elite policymaking into public view. It helped reify the role of disability activists advocating on their own behalf, championing a message of empowerment. Visible protest almost always had a dual goal: one tied to specific objectives like preventing budget cuts or ending a fundraising telethon; the other to expose the efforts of a constituency seeking to mitigate inequalities. In examining the three waves of disability protest, it is hard to miss the long-lasting impacts of visible protest on the movement.

Today, the disability movement draws from its past as well as contemporary progressive activism. Like BLM and the Women's March, which connected the experiences of the Black civil rights movement and feminism to contemporary intersectional activism (Berry and Chenoweth 2018; Ray 2020), the disability movement increasingly focuses on economic injustices and inequality. Forging ties with broader activist networks and adjacent cause fields has done much to motivate the use of protest in the disability rights movement. Although grievances at their core have changed relatively little, disability activists continue to use visible protests to draw attention to the social barriers that perpetuate intersectional forms of inequality. With each protest wave, activists used visible protests to get the message out about why and how things need to change.

5 Waves of Continuity and Change

The disability rights movement saw comparatively fewer visible protests than the LGBT movement, women's movement, Black civil rights, and reproductive rights (King, Bentele, and Soule 2007). Perhaps this is because of the disability movement's origins in more institutional work which saw seemingly key legislative successes and support from elites early on. The movement has been referred to as a "silent army" and a "quiet revolution" (Diamond 1973; Abeson and Zettell 1977). Yet, as I described in this volume, visible protest had important material, psychological, and symbolic rewards for activists and the disability rights movement. Why did visible and disruptive protests emerge at all?

---

[120] Militant Advocacy Group for Disabled Revels in Role as Agitator, *New York Times*, October 10, 1991.

People with disabilities were increasingly organizing into a political constituency and increasingly seen that way by political elites. This would have long-term impacts on the disability cause field. Upward policy trajectories and positive feedback effects resulted from this group mobilizing to protect policies. This effectively meant that people with disabilities were no longer just seen as passive recipients of social services; they were citizens actively protecting their policy and political interests (Campbell 2003).

Exogenous forces like the "minority rights revolution" (Skrentny 2002) and the rise of professional advocacy (Minkoff 1999; Staggenborg and Taylor 2005) created new institutional and cultural circumstances within which people with disabilities could situate their long-standing grievances. As Heumann explained at her 2018 Ted Talk, "we were learning from the Civil Rights Movement and from the Women's Rights Movement. We were learning from them about their activism and their ability to come together, not only to discuss problems but to discuss solutions. And what was born is what we call today the Disability Rights Movement."

As I show here, there will always be grievances upon which to mobilize and part of the reason why is that outcomes are often partial and plagued by backtracking that undoes any potential resolutions. Grievances tied to the numerous issue areas mobilizing disability activists, while experiencing different levels of prominence, tended to be relatively constant across waves. Although grievances help inform what protests are about, political and social movement dynamics dictate what the goals of protest should be, what its targets are, and what protest should accomplish. In each wave, disability organizations and activist networks adapted to hybrid environments of opportunity and threat (McAdam et al. 2010) as part of the issue politics they contended with. Mobilization and issue politics are related in non-recursive ways – they are both cycles reflecting a back-and-forth between progress and retrenchment and the ambiguities surrounding short-term and long-term partial victories leaving issues open.

Connecting grievances and issue areas over time as I have done here provides a necessary context for exploring protest waves. Doing so sheds light on the relationship between discontent, opportunity, and threat, the connection between regular and contentious politics, the role of SMOs and activist networks, and the outcomes of collective action that go on to shape subsequent cycles of protest. Protest waves are not independent of one another. Although waves of mobilization are best understood within the specific cultural and institutional contexts within which they emerge and decline (Gillan 2020), these environments also reflect the outcomes of prior mobilizing efforts. By outcomes, I mean not only whether intended protest goals were satisfied or not, but also the cultural, organizational, and tactical developments that influenced subsequent protest (Staggenborg 1995; Tarrow 1989). Indeed, protest not only shapes subsequent protest, but it also transforms cause fields by changing power balances, structures, culture, relationships, and constituency demands.

Collective action leading up to the Resistance including Occupy, BLM, and climate justice have made racism, classism, sexism, and ableism relevant to today's cultural and political context while building on past movement efforts. Both Whittier (2018) and Oliver (2020) point to preexisting structures that helped facilitate the Resistance. The Resistance included formal and informal networks of activists who over the last decade, had already been mobilizing against inequality via Occupy, Standing Rock, and BLM and through formal advocacy groups like the ACLU and NAACP (Berry and Chenoweth 2018). Political organizing around Hillary Clinton's campaign as well as existing groups like Emily's List and NOW, as Whittier explains, were "poised for action." Resisters relied on similar organizational forms and tactics – "following well-worn paths" (Whitter 2018:226). Visible protests organized by DIA, ADAPT, and ACCD in the 1980s and 1990s laid the groundwork for the Resistance, Rise and Resist, and the disability Non-March. These groups and activist networks identified opportunities and responded to threats, supplied frames, and provided tactical experience (Earl, Copeland, and Bimber 2017; McAdam 2017).

This growing tide had important impacts on the disability movement as new opportunities arose for activists to bring existing grievances back into the mainstream of American politics in an up-to-date way. Neither disability activism nor the specific issue of homecare is new but 23-year-old disability activist, Kings Floyd who has muscular dystrophy and participated in the Women's March, revived her local ADAPT chapter in 2018.[121] Floyd was motivated by Trump and GOP threats to homecare and Medicaid funding. Floyd was among the new and long-time activists coming together in protest, like Anita Cameron. Cameron has apparently been arrested 130 times at past ADAPT protests. She said that this time, "It's far more intense. We really feel our lives are at stake."

Efforts to change the nursing home Medicaid funding bias is an issue area that simultaneously showcases the successes of a social movement in raising awareness about injustice within the politics of American healthcare reform, and ongoing challenges in bringing about meaningful institutional change. Community-based care has become a fixture for the disability rights movement because underlying grievances are tied to structural obstacles that have seen little by way of significant reforms. Since the early 1980s, policymakers have

---

[121] https://time.com/5168472/disability-activism-trump/.

offered partial solutions for homecare avoiding the hard political work of transforming Social Security (Pettinicchio 2023). Some of those outcomes were in part a result of disruptive visible protests and other more institutional tactics. With each partial solution, activists on the one hand found new opportunities to mobilize around homecare but on the other, were subsequently met with disappointment when those efforts did not lead to meaningful long-term reforms.

The disability rights movement provides key lessons about how issues, grievances, tactics, and responses to mobilization evolve, and about what activists may or may not gain using visible protests. Issues and grievances seldom just disappear. Even when individual protests appear to be making inroads, grievances are redefined and evolve alongside new developments within issue areas, which can include threats and backtracking. Examining mobilizing efforts across issue areas provides more insight into how protest waves are connected in time and space. Finally, as I show in this work, identifying the outcomes of protest as a response to opportunity and threat is critical for understanding change and continuity across protest waves. At the same time, my analysis raises further questions about whether and how activists are thought to achieve their goals in the short- and long term and what this means for the ebb and flow of protest.

5.1 The Decline of Visible Protest Waves

In the 1990s and 2000s, disability visible protests as well as the use of more institutionalized tactics saw a steady decline. One possible explanation for this may be some form of issue closure. The years leading up to the 1990 ADA reflected what seemed like major legislative victories. However, these policies failed to deliver in a variety of areas from increasing employment opportunities to preventing needless institutionalization to securing resources for both mainstream and special education – core grievances for the disability movement.

The constellation of factors that shape demobilization are complex and movement scholars are often confronted with the unenviable task of accounting for the numerous reasons why protest waves subside. One reason for demobilization likely has something to do with outcomes – whether activists are met with repression, stalemates, or victories (partial or full).

Partial victories and partial gains may reflect partial solutions. The problem with half solutions is that they coopt underlying root problems by yielding to "easy fixes" (Campbell 2003; Coy and Hedeen 2005). As such, partial victories may leave extant grievances in place and generate discontent later on. At the same time, when partial solutions are an attempt by elites to manage conflict, they can leave movements in disarray and unprepared to strike back if half solutions indeed leave issues unresolved and/or generate new areas of concern. The disability movement is rife with examples of limited immediate gains, and significant obstacles in obtaining longer-term reforms. And, even when mobilization leads to full success, those achievements are not inherently protected from backtracking – another broader lesson learned from studying the cycle of American policymaking (Pettinicchio 2019).

Of course, making connections between action and outcomes is often done in hindsight. Demobilization can be a long process as it involves many actors, institutions, groups, and broader political environments (Sawyers and Meyer 1999). As sophisticated as activists may be, it is not always obvious what responses to mobilization will mean in the short or long term, and activists and groups must draw from experience to figure that out.

Decline in protest activity is often used as a proxy for overall movement demobilization. Institutionalization, cooptation, organizational maintenance, strategic shifts, and activist disengagement, have all been broadly associated with demobilization (Bosi 2016; Piven and Cloward 1977). Decline in protest may be related to exogenous forces like shifts in political opportunities and issue presence on the policy agenda which also ebbs and flows (see Baumgartner and Jones 1993). These determine the kinds of access challengers have to elites. Maher et al. (2019) recently found that for protest, access to elites matter early in a movement and less later, whereas movement organizations may matter more for protest in periods of decline and when access to elites is more constrained. This may be because organizations can more efficiently seek out narrower windows of opportunity and maintain interest among activists. Koopmans (2004) suggested that the routinization of interaction between challengers and elites leads to a decline in visible protests, presumably because protest is less useful (and potentially more harmful) when movement organizations and activists already have their ear. Still, like grievances, routine access to elites does not fully account for why disability protest waves ebbed and flowed especially because disability visible protest occurred when activists had both greater and less access to elites. Whatever the case, the literature points to some interaction between elites, opportunities, and organizations in explaining the use of institutional and extra-institutional tactics.

When we discount demobilization, we may underestimate political action if movement activity continues in other forms that are less visible (Amenta, Andrews, and Caren 2019). As Oliver, Lim, and Matthews (2022) suggest, movements that are not orchestrating visible protests may not be demobilizing entirely. Visible protests in some areas may also be displaced by more institutional tactics or movement building efforts that may be important later for subsequent waves. Visible protest may also decline at different paces depending on issue areas. In some cases, protests may see an uptick in some areas, while others see decline. This paints a messier picture of protest cycles and requires thinking more about how factors associated with increases in protests work similarly or differently on protest's decline (Demirel-Pegg 2017).

One way to begin approaching this, as I have done here, is to situate the use of visible protest alongside other forms of movement activity that are less visible, like lobbying and legal mobilization. This is useful for shedding light on protest cycles because it demonstrates a broader tactical repertoire and nuanced relationship between challengers and elites. Even when activists had routine access to elites, they adapted to their targets of action (see Della Porta and Parks 2014). Part of the way they adapt is by identifying new opportunities and strategies as issue politics evolve (Staggenborg 2013) which could mean increasing protest activity, increasing the use of more institutional tactics, or both. Groups and activists are tactically flexible as I show in each of the three disability protest waves, combining disruption with "regular politics."

5.2 The Symbolic Meaning of Protest

I examined visible protests over an extended period within a single movement that mobilized across numerous issue areas. This approach helped to connect movement goals, targets, and tactics when the use of visible protest was at its highest as well as at its lowest (Lewin 2019; Staggenborg and Taylor 2005). Many of the visible protest events included in this data were associated with other less visible forms of action, which had direct bearing on the structure of a social movement, its relationship with its targets, and to the outcomes of protest. Despite claims that a potential consequence of professionalization and institutionalization is a reluctance to engage in more disruptive action (Earl 2013; Staggenborg 1988), the disability movement highlights the ways in which activists and groups bend with the wind (Minkoff 1999; Staggenborg 2015).

ADAPT grew out of an informal network of activists and became more formalized and professionalized. DIA too was formed by activists who already had political experience and some ties with political elites.

Groups like ADAPT, DIA, and PVA all engaged in a mix of tactics, albeit in varying degrees. And, as in past protest waves, activists, and groups, like for example, the AAPD, continue using visible disruptive protest as well as more institutional tactics including voter registration drives like #cripthevote which began in 2016, and supporting disabled people running for elected office. Tactical flexibility reflects a conscious strategy on the part of activists and SMOs when it comes to targets and goals (Meyer and Staggenborg 2012).

Tactical flexibility is critical given the dynamic nature of hybrid environments of threat and opportunity which shape the ongoing relationship between activists and elites. Threats from those with resources and power emerge even when movements find sympathetic elite allies to work with. Threat can therefore trigger visible protests while movement groups and activists maintain regular political channels open. This helps account for why many visible disability protests were also associated with more institutional tactics before, during, and following protest events. Clearly, some disability activists believed institutional tactics worked to get things done and the analysis I presented here bears that out. But many activists at different points in time and across different issues areas also saw institutional tactics as insufficient in obtaining meaningful change.

Disability protests were seen as effective in signaling why, when, and how change must come about (Tilly 2004; Wouters and Walgrave 2017). Addressing what activists want out of protest requires thinking more about the objective and subjective understandings of protest's success and failure. Defining success is somewhat elusive in studies of social movements (Gamson 1975; Oberschall 1993; Staggenborg 2015; Staggenborg and Meyer 2022). Even once objectives and outcomes can be clearly identified, it is still difficult to disentangle whether movement efforts directly or indirectly shaped those outcomes (Amenta, Andrews, and Caren 2019; see Johnson, Agnone, and McCarthy 2010; King, Bentele, and Soule 2007; Olzak and Soule 2009 on protest's effect on policy change and agenda setting)

With the nursing home/homecare fight, where activists sought to make major policy inroads but generally were unsuccessful, disruptive protests were organized purposely to be dramatic[122] drawing attention to the issue. For example, activists placed crosses on the White House north lawn each representing people with disabilities who died because of substandard care in nursing homes. They were trying to make a point, just as they did when they protested at New York Governor Cuomo's home on the same issue.[123] Protests do "signifying work" (McAdam 1996) in part by building unity and increasing the worthiness and legitimacy of the cause (Wouters 2019). They may also indirectly shape policy by shaping voter attitudes.

Perhaps for those reasons, activists and SMOs focused protest efforts on changing attitudes and increasing disability representation, rather than policymakers and policy, especially in the third protest wave. These efforts were key in making disruptive protests part of the movement's repertoire, as disruptive

---

[122] A Cry for Freedom and an Outcry Over the Killings, *Washington Post*, May 10, 1993.
[123] Disability Group Makes Point, *Washington Post*, June 20, 2000.

protest became more accessible to activists. Visible protests also increased authenticity among groups and networks representing disability interests (Walker and Stepick 2020). First-wave protests were associated with newer groups like DIA that distinguished themselves from existing disability groups (like Easter Seals and March of Dimes) in part by using disruptive action. In that sense, protests came to have a particular symbolic meaning to disability activists.

By the second wave, protest had come to distinguish some groups as "real" SMOs from other "relics." Visible protest had also become a way for activists to express discontent within their own cause field when they believed groups like PVA, Easter Seals, and Goodwill, Lighthouse for the Blind, and Autism Speaks were promoting problematic, outdated, and harmful views of disability. Visible protests also established that SMOs and activists were not coopted by elites simply because they had routine access to them. Groups challenged those same elites through disruption when they were not making any gains or felt threatened. Extending beyond the disability movement, the dynamic between insiders and outsiders and between institutional and extra-institutional activism is a feature of modern-day movements; mobilization is multipronged and multifaceted.

5.3 Concluding Remarks

In this volume, I provided a macro portrait of disability protests over a sixty-year period addressing how visible protest mattered for the disability rights movement at different times during its life course. I also zoomed in on the distinct but often intersecting issue areas which make up the bigger cause field within which protest is situated. Social movements inhabit these institutional and cultural environments (Bereni 2021) which inherently include interactions among actors inside and outside movements (Fligstein and McAdam 2012; Pettinicchio 2013). Cause fields emphasize a relational structure among a variety of targets, goals, tactics, and activists and organizations, and outcomes, providing context for understanding how visible protest can be both a cause and a consequence of structural and cultural developments (Meyer 2005, 2007). In this work, I provided a more detailed picture of protest's rise and fall, when protest matters, who it matters for, and for what.

The coevolution of issue areas and mobilization points to both continuity and change. Long-standing grievances surrounding access to care, inaccessible public transit, employment discrimination, and lack of educational resources reflect movement successes and failures. Sustained grievances coupled with partial victories embedded in a hybrid environment of opportunity and threat showcase how protests are shaped by their unique historical moments, but also by the politics and mobilization that came before. As I showed here, each disability protest wave is inherently defined in part by the dynamic between challengers and elites via organizations, tactics, goals, and outcomes that preceded it. And second and third waves of protest were most certainly shaped by the experience, resources, and opportunities generated by the first protest wave. Protest waves, as distinct as they may be, are not independent of one another.

I referred frequently to the Resistance throughout my analysis. As Fisher et al. (2018) explained, the Resistance is another recent example like climate activism and BLM of how everyday people turn to disruptive action when they do not feel heard. The Resistance is an historical moment – a contemporary example of mass mobilization within which new and long-time disability activists and groups sought to address many of the same kinds of grievances that mobilized prior generations.

The Resistance points to at least two key processes my analysis highlights: the role of threat in generating protest waves; and continuity and change in issue areas. The rise of Trump signaled new threats to constituencies. As Professor and paralympic medalist Anjali Forber-Pratt put it, "Trump's policies are playing an important role in identity development."[124] Threats are contingent on the politics and actors of the time. But the impact of threat on mobilization is generalizable. Nixon in the 1970s and Reagan in the 1980s brought their own brand of threat to which activists mobilized as they sought to thwart retrenchment efforts while creating new opportunities for future waves to secure resources for the disability cause. In all three periods, disability activists and groups used visible protest, institutional tactics, and joined broader coalitions in response to threats. They all experienced a mix of outcomes.

Disability groups were responding to threats, but they were also exploiting evolving opportunities around a set of grievances that remain fixtures in disability politics (Meyer 2004; Van Dyke and Soule 2002). The coevolution of issue politics and movement mobilization explains how grievances regain saliency and how new iterations evolve to mobilize a greater number of activists that cut across cause fields, like the Resistance (Fisher, Dow, and Ray 2017; McKane and McCammon 2018; Whittier 2018).

When focusing on any one specific historical moment or wave of mobilization, we may gravitate to its newness. But protest does not just materialize out of the blue. Protests are neither acontextual nor are they ahistorical. In the case of the more recent wave of disability mobilization via the Resistance, protest emerged from a preexisting organizational and network base cutting across

---

[124] 'Our Lives Are at Stake.' How Donald Trump Inadvertently Sparked a New Disability Rights Movement, *Time Magazine*, February 26, 2018.

strategic action fields. Recent mass mobilization emphasizes how protest events are connected to past efforts, as well as within and across different movements and cause fields. In other words, protests are connected across both time and space. They impact culture and institutions in the long term, and in doing so, reshape grievances, goals, and activists' objectives along the way.

Looking at sixty years of visible disability protests was necessary for capturing cycles of mobilization around perennial issues. What my analysis in part reveals is that issues, threats, and grievances are not new. Even the visible protests organized by disability activists during the Resistance were not novel as much as they were a turning point in an otherwise protracted struggle, much like the protest waves that emerged at the close of the 1980s and again in the late 2000s. In the case of disability, movement targets often dismissed grievances, or worse yet, made grievances and demands seem ridiculous and unreasonable. They often excluded voices of people with disabilities in decision-making and, provided short-term half solutions to manage conflict. They left issues unresolved, facilitating efforts to undermine the disability community further still. And, threat does not just go away. Like issue and protest cycles, threat ebbs and flows as an important dimension of the political process generalizable to a host of cause fields which have experienced bursts of progress followed by backstepping. Politics surrounding reproductive rights, race, and gender have all recently seen activists respond to threats and new opportunities to forge alliances and reinvigorate mass action. As Andrews, Caren, and Browne (2018) explain, the very success of the Resistance lies in how these broad alliances contributed to the size, sustainability, and visibility of mobilization. Disability activism contributed to that success.

As with past waves, the last five years too represent a hybrid environment of threat and opportunity. Activists helped bring disability into contemporary mainstream American politics while challenging allies to do better when it came to disability inclusion. In many ways, disability activists followed BIPOC activists in carving out spaces within organizations and networks that serve as contemporary foundations for protest. Jennifer Bartlett was not only mobilizing activists against external threats. She was also fighting for disability representation on the Women's March Alliance's board. Katherine Siemionko of the Alliance denied the group was actively excluding disabled people and sent a cease and desist to Bartlett. Eventually, Bartlett and RAR endorsed the New York Women's March and changed the timing of their event to allow activists to attend both.[125] It was a success, and for protesters like Bartlett, it was

---

[125] How New York City Ended up with Two Competing Women's Marches, *New York Times*, January 16, 2019.

an opportunity to show what disability activism was about and what their contribution to social change has been and will continue to be.

Visible protest, as one disability movement leader put it, moved disability from symbolic acceptance to real acceptance.[126] Where structural changes lacked, activists sought to change public attitudes about disability. Activists brought their message to the American people. Visible protest went a long way in publicizing disability as an axis of inequality like race, class, and gender; that disability is a minority group; that what must change is not disabled people, but unjust and ableist institutions and cultures that oppress, exclude, and disadvantage. What's next for the disability rights movement? Right now, disability mobilization is more robust and diverse than ever. As it adapts to dynamic political and cultural circumstances, it continues its efforts in shaping institutions as well as public attitudes.

---

[126] Congressional Hearing: 80-S541-25, 1979.

Appendix

This project builds on an original disability protest dataset ($n = 172$ events) covering the period between 1961 and 2006 across four newspapers (*New York Times, Los Angeles Times, Washington Post,* and *San Francisco Chronicle*) (see Pettinicchio 2019 for more information). With the help of a graduate research assistant at the University of Toronto, Andy Holmes, the data was extended to include fifteen more years of protest data (2007–2021) resulting in sixty-two new distinct protest events, for a total of 234 events. The last fifteen years is important because it covers the emergence of a third wave of protest following a lengthy period of decline in visible disability protest throughout the 1990s and early 2000s. This more recent period of mobilization covers long-standing issues like homecare, accessibility, and social welfare cuts, as well as relatively newer issues like inclusion and diversity efforts, and media portrayals of disability. It also takes into account the movement context of the 2010 and 2020s, including the rise of Occupy, BLM, and the Resistance.

These newspapers by and large report on regional and national events. I include the *San Francisco Chronicle* because the Bay Area is a known disability movement center and because, along with the LA Times, the paper covered events on the west coast. Accessing the SFC since 2011 was more complicated due to licensing agreements. However, I purchased archival access for 2012–2021 directly through the SFC with a research fund generously provided by the Department of Sociology at the University of Toronto. Focusing on full daily issues of four newspapers ensures consistency across papers and across time. Using search terms in databases like Newsbank (for example) overestimates the number of disability-related protests (Barnartt 2010). My original content analysis produced a distribution of disability protests very similar to that reported by King, Bentele, and Soule (2007).

Coverage of protests provides important information across several key variables. Borrowing from Oliver and Myers (1999), size is coded as Small/Modest (less than 99), Medium (100–499) Large (500–999) Very Large (greater than 1000) based on estimated numbers reported. Duration is coded in terms of the number of hours the protest lasted as reported by the article: Short (less than 1 day/5–24 hours), Moderate (1 day/24 hours), Long (2–3 days/48–72 hours), Very Long (4 days or more/ >96 hours). Arrests were infrequently reported (about 16 percent). Targets of protest were coded into four main types: local and state government (e.g., Anaheim city council, Virginia State Chamber of Commerce), federal government (e.g., Reagan administration, HEW), and private/public corporations and organizations (e.g., Greyhound Bus, US Airways, New York

MTA, and CBS). The goals of protest are sometimes explicitly noted in the article, although often, goals had to be inferred. There were four broad types of goals: more/better services, implement/expand/stop cuts to rights, increase spending /stop funding cuts, and raise awareness about disability portrayals (see Table A.1).

The newspaper article is itself not the observation of interest. Rather, it is the distinct protest event it reports on. Although information for each disability protest event is based on an account provided in one of the four newspapers content analyzed in this study, each protest event was also cross-referenced to ensure the fullest description of the event possible. This means that multiple newspaper accounts, documents found online, as well as reports by organizations and activists about the events were analyzed to corroborate any one single account.

This was also especially important for determining whether goals as stated by leaders and activists in these accounts were achieved. For example, numerous protests were about demanding meetings with officials which they sometimes got, and other times did not. This was usually reported within the news article. Many protests around spending cuts had no immediate resolution and typically were unsuccessful in deterring cuts as reflected in next year's budget. Some protests where activists demanded accessibility led to cooperation but also to foot-dragging and noncompliance by targets. Therefore, getting at goal achievement required extending the analysis beyond the event to determine outcomes. This also helped to show the complicated nature of determining success and failure. For instance, in a protest event on education cuts that specifically would harm disadvantaged students with disabilities in elementary schools, protesters were able to get the board to withdraw the proposal before the final budget vote. In the long run though, the board also indicated that they would re-evaluate special needs programs suggesting a potential temporary victory. Similarly, learning about goal achievement in a protest in May of 1993 around keeping a special education center opened required researching the outcome beyond the May news coverage. The center was indeed closed in June of that year.

The focus of this project is on direct action – specifically, the coordination of and participation in disruptive visible forms of collective action. However, an important aspect of this project is to situate protest within a broader context and repertoire of political action. As such, I drew from existing and updated data on the participation of organizations in congressional hearings (which often occurred alongside protest events), as well as their involvement with key court cases (cases which were often directly or indirectly the subject of visible protest, see Pettinicchio 2019). This provides a more holistic schema of the way activists and groups use different tactics and what they intend to gain from their usage.

Table A.1 Describing visible disability protest events (*n* = 234)

		Cases	Percent
Target	Federal	77	32.9
	State	51	21.8
	Local	54	23.1
	Business/Organizations	52	22.2
	Non-Disability Specific Event	55	23.5
Goal	More/Better Services	27	11.5
	Implement/Expand/Stop Cuts to Rights	75	32.1
	Increase Spending / Stop Cuts	107	45.7
	Raise Awareness about Portraying Disability	25	10.7
Issue Area	Employment	6	2.6
	Transportation	44	18.8
	Healthcare	63	26.9
	Education	23	9.8
	Social Welfare	58	24.8
	Discrimination	24	10.3
	Media/Cultural Sites	16	6.8
Other Activities	Working with policy/decision makers	30	20.4
	Testifying/Participating in Hearings/Lobbying	83	56.5
	Litigation/ Legal Counsel/Court Cases	29	19.7
	Other	5	3.4
Organizational Involvement	At least one disability group	155	66.2
	More than one disability group	33	14.1
	Presence of at least one non-disability group	77	32.9

Table A.1 (cont.)

		Cases	Percent
Events with Arrests/ Citations		39	16.7
	No	113	48.3
Goal Achieved	Partial	66	28.2
	Full	55	23.5
Duration in hours ($n = 164$)			
Mean			270.4
Median			24
Size in number of participants ($n = 215$)			
Mean			4231.4
Median			100

References

Abeson, A., and Zettel, J. (1977). "The End of Quiet Revolution: The Education for All Handicapped Children Act of 1975." *Exceptional Children*, 44(2), 114–128.

Abramovitz, M. (2004). "Saving Capitalism from Itself: Whither the Welfare State?." *New England Journal of Public Policy*, 20 (1), Article 6.

Almeida, P. (2019). *Social Movements: The Structure of Collective Mobilization*. Berkeley, CA: University of California Press.

Amenta, E., Andrews, K. T., and Caren, K. (2019). "The Political Institutions, Processes, and Outcomes Movements Seek to Influence." In D. A. Snow, S. A. Soule, H. Kriesi, and H. McCammon (Eds.), *The Wiley Blackwell Companion to Social Movements*, 2nd ed. San Francisco, CA: John Wiley.

Andrews, K. T., Caren, N., and Browne, A. (2018). "Protesting Trump." *Mobilization: An International Quarterly*, 23(4), 393–400.

Avila-Saavedra, G. (2009). "Nothing Queer about Queer Television: Televised Construction of Gay Masculinities." *Media, Culture, & Society*, 31(1), 5–21.

Barnartt, S. (2010). "The Globalization of Disability Protests, 1970–2005: Pushing the Limits of Cross- Cultural Research?." *Comparative Sociology*, 9(2), 222–240.

Baumgartner, F. R., and Jones, B. D. (1993). *Agendas and Instability in American Politics*. Chicago, IL: University of Chicago Press.

Bereni, L. (2021) "The Women's Cause in a Field: Rethinking the Architecture of Collective Protest in the Era of Movement Institutionalization." *Social Movement Studies*, 20(2), 208–223.

Berry, M., and Erica, C. (2018). "Who Made the Women's March?" In D. S. Meyer, and S. Tarrow (Eds.), *The Resistance: The Dawn of the Anti-Trump Opposition Movement* (pp. 75–88). New York: Oxford University Press.

Bosi, L. (2016). "Incorporation and Democratization: The Long-term Process of Institutionalization of the Northern Ireland Civil Rights Movement." In L. Bosi, M. Giugni, and K. Uba (Eds.), *The Consequences of Social Movements* (pp. 338–360). Cambridge: Cambridge University Press.

Campbell, A. L. (2003). *How Policies Make Citizens: Senior Political Activism and the American Welfare State*. Princeton, NJ: Princeton University Press.

Carey, A., Block, P., and Scotch, R. (2020). *Allies and Obstacles*. Philadelphia, PA: Temple University Press.

Christiansen, J. B., and Barnartt, S. (1988). *Deaf President Now! The 1988 Revolution at Gallaudet University*. Washington, DC: Gallaudet University Press.

Corcoran, K. E., Pettinicchio, D., and Young, J. T. N. (2011). "The Context of Control: A Cross-national Investigation of the Link between Political Institutions, Efficacy, and Collective Action." *British Journal of Social Psychology*, 50(4), 575–605.

Coy, P. G., and Tim, H. (2005). "A Stage Model of Social Movement Co-optation: Community Mediation in the United States." *Sociological Quarterly*, 46(3), 405–435.

Della Porta, D. (2011)."Eventful Protest, Global Conflicts: Social Mechanisms in the Reproduction of Protest." In J. Jasper and J. Goodwin (Eds.), *Contention in Context: Political Opportunities and the Emergence of Protest* (pp. 256–276). Stanford, CA: Stanford University Press.

Della Porta, D. (2022). "Progressive Social Movements and the Creation of European Public Spheres." *Theory, Culture, & Society*, 39(4), 51–65.

Della Porta, D., and Alcie, M. (2014). *Spreading Protest: Social Movements in Times of Crisis*. Colchester: ECPR Press, Studies in European Political Science Series.

Della Porta, D., and Parks, L. (2014). "Framing Processes in the Climate Movement: From Climate Change to Climate Justice." In M. Dietz and H. Garrelts (Eds.), *Routledge Handbook of the Climate Change Movement* (pp.19-30). London: Routledge Press.

Demirel-Pegg, T. (2017). "The Dynamics of the Demobilization of the Protest Campaign in Assam." *International Interactions*, 43(2), 175–216.

Dimond, P. R. (1973). "The Constitutional Right to Education: The Quiet Revolution." *Hastings Law Journal*, 24, 1087–1127.

Earl, J. (2013). "Spreading the Word or Shaping the Conversation: 'Prosumption' in Protest Websites." *Research in Social Movements, Conflicts, and Change*, 36, 3–38.

Earl, J., Copeland, L., and Bimber, B. (2017). "Routing around Organizations: Self-directed Political Consumption." *Mobilization*, 22(2), 131–153.

Earl, J., Soule, S. A., and McCarthy, J. D. (2003). "Protest under Fire? Explaining the Policing of Protest." *American Sociological Review*, 68(4), 581–606.

Elliott, T., Earl, J., Maher, T. V., and Reynolds-Stenson, H. (2022). "Softer Policing or the Institutionalization of Protest? Decomposing Changes in Observed Protest Policing over Time." *American Journal of Sociology*, 127(4), 1311–1365.

Evans, P. B., Sewell, W. H., Jr. (2013). " Neoliberalism: Policy Regimes, International Regimes, and Social Effects." In P. A. Halland and M. Lamont (Eds.), *Social Resilience in the Neoliberal Era* (pp. 35–68). Cambridge: Cambridge University Press.

Fisher, D., and Nasrin, S. (2021). "Shifting Coalitions within the Youth Climate Movement in the US." *Politics and Governance*, 9(2), 112–123.

Fisher, D. R., Jasny, L., and Dow, D. M. (2018). "Why Are We Here? Patterns of Intersectional Motivations across the Resistance." *Mobilization*, 23(4), 45–68.

Fisher, D., Dow, D. M., and Ray, R. (2017). "Intersectionality Takes It to the Streets: Mobilizing across Diverse Interests for the Women's March." *Science Advances*, 3, 9. https://doi.org/10.1126/sciadv.aao139.www.ncbi.nlm.nih.gov/pmc/articles/PMC5606706/pdf/aao1390.pdf.

Fligstein, N., and McAdam, D. (2012). *A Theory of Fields*. Oxford: Oxford University Press.

Foster, J., and Pettinicchio, D. (2022). "A Model Who Looks Like Me: Communicating and Consuming Representations of Disability." *Journal of Consumer Culture*, 22(3), 579–597.

Friedman C. (2019). "Ableism, Racism, and Subminimum Wage in the United States." *Disability Studies Quarterly*, 39(4), 1–21.

Gamson, W. A. (1975). *The Strategy of Social Protest*. Belmont, CA: Wadsworth Press.

Gamson, W. A. (2004). "Bystanders, Public Opinion, and the Media." In D. A. Snow, S. A. Soule and H. Kriesi (Eds.), *The Blackwell Companion to Social Movements* (pp. 242–261). Malden, MA: Blackwell.

Garland-Thomson, R. (2002). "Integrating Disability, Transforming Feminist Theory." *NWSA Journal*, 14(3), 1–32.

Gillan, K. (2020). "Temporality in Social Movement Theory: Vectors and Events in the Neoliberal Timescape." *Social Movement Studies*, 19(5–6), 516–536.

Goldstone, J. A. (1980). "The Weakness of Organization: A New Look at Gamson's": The Strategy of Social Protest. *American Journal of Sociology*, 85, 1917–1942.

Johnson, E. W., Agnone, J., and McCarthy, J. D. (2010). "Movement Organization, Synergistic Tactics and Environmental Public Policy." *Social Forces*, 88(5), 2267–2292.

Katzmann, R. A. (1986). *Institutional Disability: The Saga of Transportation Policy for the Disabled*. Washington, DC: Brookings Institution.

Ketchley, N., and El-Rayyes, T. (2021). "Unpopular Protest: Mass Mobilization and Attitudes to Democracy in Post-Mubarak Egypt." *The Journal of Politics*, 83(1), 291–305.

King, B. G., Bentele, K. G., and Soule, S. A. (2007). "Protest and Policymaking: Explaining Fluctuation in Congressional Attention to Rights Issues, 1960–1986." *Social Forces*, 86(1), 137–164.

Koopmans, R. (2004). "Protest in Time and Space: The Evolution of Waves of Contention." In D. A. Snow, S. A. Soule, and H. Kriesi (Eds.), *The Blackwell Companion to Social Movements* (pp. 19–46). Oxford: Blackwell.

Lewin, P. (2019). "'I Just Keep My Mouth Shut': The Demobilization of Environmental Protest in Central Appalachia." *Social Currents*, 6(6), 534–552.

Longmore, P. K. (2015). *Telethons: Spectacle, Disability, and the Business of Charity.* New York: Oxford University Press.

Maher, T. V., Martin, A., McCarthy, J. D., and Moorhead, L. (2019). "Assessing the Explanatory Power of Social Movement Theories across the Life Course of the Civil Rights Movement." *Social Currents*, 6(5), 399–421.

Maroto, M., and Pettinicchio, D. (2014). "The Limitations of Disability Antidiscrimination Legislation: Policymaking and the Economic Well-being of People with Disabilities." *Law & Policy*, 36, 370–407.

Maroto, M., and Pettinicchio, D. (2022). "Worth Less? Exploring the Effects of Subminimum Wages on Poverty among U.S. Hourly Workers." *Sociological Perspectives*, 66(3), 455–475. https://doi.org/10.1177/07311214221124630.

Mauldin, L., and Brown, R. L. (2021). "Missing Pieces: Engaging Sociology of Disability in Medical Sociology." *Journal of Health and Social Behavior*, 62(4), 477–492.

McAdam, D. (1996). "Conceptual Origins, Current Problems, Future Directions." In D. McAdam, J. D. McCarthy, and M. N. Zald (Eds.), *Comparative Perspectives on Social Movements: Political Opportunity Structures, Mobilizing Structures, and Cultural Framings* (pp. 23–40). Cambridge: Cambridge University Press.

McAdam, D. (2017). "Social Movement Theory and the Prospects for Climate Change Activism in the United States." *Annual Review of Political Science*, 20(1), 189–208.

McAdam, D., Boudet, H. S., Davis, J. et al. (2010). "'Site Fights': Explaining Opposition to Pipeline Projects in the Developing World." *Sociological Forum*, 25, 401–427.

McKane, R. G., and McCammon, H. J. (2018). "Why We March: The Role of Grievances, Threats, and Movement Organizational Resources in the 2017 Women's Marches." *Mobilization: An International Quarterly*, December 1, 23(4), 401–424.

Melucci, A. (1996). *Challenging Codes: Collective Action in the Information Age* (Cambridge Cultural Social Studies). Cambridge: Cambridge University Press.

Meyer, D. S. (2004). "Protest and Political Opportunities." *Annual Review of Sociology*, 30(1), 125–145.

Meyer, D. S. (2005). "Social Movements and Public Policy: Eggs, Chicken, and Theory." In D. Meyer, V. Jenness, and H. Ingram (Eds.), *Routing the Opposition: Social Movements, Public Policy, and Democracy* (pp. 1–26). Minneapolis, MN: University of Minnesota Press.

Meyer, D. S. (2007). *The Politics of Protest: Social Movements in America.* New York: Oxford University Press.

Meyer, D. S., and Minkoff, D. C. (2004). "Conceptualizing Political Opportunity." *Social Forces*, 82(4), 1457–1492.

Meyer, D. S., and Staggenborg, S. (2012). "Thinking about Strategy." In G. M. Maney, R. V. Kutz- Flamenbaum, and D. A. Rohlinger (Eds.), *Strategies for Social Change* (pp. 3–22). Minneapolis, MN: University of Minnesota Press.

Minkoff, D. C. (1999). "Bending with the Wind: Strategic Chance and Adaptation by Women's and Racial Minority Organizations." *American Journal of Sociology*, 104(6), 1666–1703.

Minkoff, D. C. (2002). "The Emergence of Hybrid Organizational Forms: Combining Identity-Based Service Provision and Political Action." *Nonprofit and Voluntary Sector Quarterly*, 31(3), 377–401.

Morris, A. (1986). *Origins of the Civil Rights Movement.* New York: The Free Press.

Oberschall, A. (1993). *Social Movements: Ideologies, Interests, and Identities.* New York: Transaction

Oliver, P. (2020). "Resisting Repression: The Black Lives Movement in Context." In H. Johnston and P. Oliver (Eds.), *Racialized Protest and the State: Resistance and Repression in a Divided America* (pp. 63-88). New York: Routledge

Oliver, P., and Myers, D. (2003). "The Coevolution of Social Movements." *Mobilization*, 8(1), 1–24.

Oliver, P., Lim, C., Matthews, M. C., and Hanna, A. (2022). "Black Protests in the United States, 1994 to 2010." *Sociological Science*, 9, 275–312.

Olzak, S., and Soule, S. A. (2009). "Cross-Cutting Influences of Environmental Protest and Legislation." *Social Forces*, 88(1), 201–225.

Opp, K.-D. (1988). "Grievances and Participation in Social Movements." *American Sociological Review*, 53(6), 853–864.

Pettinicchio, D. (2017). "Elites, Policy, and Social Movements." In B. Wejnert and P. Parigi (Eds.), *Research in Political Sociology*, Vol. 24, (pp. 155–190). Bingley: Emerald.

Pettinicchio, D. (2012). "Institutional Activism: Reconsidering the Insider/ Outsider Dichotomy." *Sociology Compass*, 6(6), 499–510.

Pettinicchio, D. (2013). "Strategic Action Fields and the Context of Political Entrepreneurship: How Disability Rights Became Part of the Policy Agenda." *Research in Social Movements, Conflicts and Change*, 36, 79–106.

Pettinicchio, D. (2019). *Politics of Empowerment: Disability Rights and the Cycle of American Policy Reform*. Stanford, CA: Stanford University Press.

Pettinicchio, D. (2023). "Tracing the Welfare-rights Connection in American Disability Policymaking." In S. Robinson and K. Fisher (Eds.), *Research Handbook of Disability Policy* (pp. 346–360). Cheltenham and Camberley, UK: Elgar.

Pfaff, S. (2006). *Exit-Voice Dynamics and the Collapse of East Germany: The Crisis of Leninism and the Revolution of 1989*. Durham, NC: Duke University Press.

Pierson, P. (1994). *Dismantling the Welfare State? Reagan, Thatcher, and the Politics of Retrenchment*. Cambridge: Cambridge University Press.

Piven, F. F., and Cloward, R. (1977). *Poor People's Movement*. New York: Pantheon Books.

Posner, P. L. (1997). "Unfunded Mandates Reform Act: 1996 and beyond." *Publius*, 27(2), 53–71.

Ray, R. (2020). "Setting the Record Straight on the Movement for Black Lives." *Ethnic and Racial Studies*, 43(8), 1–9.

Raynor, O., and Hayward, K. (2009). "Breaking into the Business: Experiences of Actors with Disabilities in the Entertainment Industry. *Journal of Research in Special Educational Needs*, 9(1), 39–47.

Rupp, L. J., and Taylor, V. A. (1987). *Survival in the Doldrums: The American Women's Rights Movement, 1945 to the 1960s*. New York: Oxford University Press.

Sawyers, T. M., and. Meyer, D. S. (1999). "Missed Opportunities: Social Movement Abeyance and Public Policy," *Social Problems*, 46(2), 187–206.

Scotch, R. K. (2001). *From Good Will to Civil Rights: Transforming Federal Disability Policy*. Philadelphia, PA: Temple University Press.

Sewell, W.H. (2005). *Logics of History*. Chicago, IL: University of Chicago Press.

Shapiro, J. P. (1993). *No Pity: People with Disabilities Forging a New Civil Rights Movement*. New York: Three Rivers Press.

Skrentny, J. D. (2002). *The Minority Rights Revolution*. Cambridge, MA: Belknap Press of Harvard University Press.

Snow, D., Cress, D., Downey, L., and Jones, A. (1998). "Disrupting the 'Quotidian': Reconceptualizing the Relationship between Breakdown and the Emergence of Collective Action." *Mobilization: An International Quarterly*, 3(1), 1–22.

Soule, S. A. (1999). "The Diffusion of an Unsuccessful Innovation." *The ANNALS of the American Academy of Political and Social Science*, 566(1), 120–131.

Soule, S. A., and Davenport, C. (2009). "Velvet Glove, Iron Fist, or Even Hand? Protest Policing in the United States, 1960–1990." *Mobilization: An International Quarterly*, 14(1), 1–22.

Soule,S., and Jennifer, E. (2005). "A Movement Society Evaluated: Collective Protest in The United States, 1960–1986." *Mobilization: An International Quarterly* 1,10(3), 345–364.

Staggenborg, S. (1986). "Coalition Work in the Pro-Choice Movement: Organizational and Environmental Opportunities and Obstacles." *Social Problems*, 33(5), 374–390.

Staggenborg, S. (1988). "The Consequences of Professionalization and Formalization in the Pro-choice Movement." *American Sociological Review*, 53(4), 585–605.

Staggenborg S. (1995). "The Survival of the Pro-choice Movement." Journal of Policy History, 7(1), 160–176.

Staggenborg, S. (2013). "Institutionalization of Social Movements." In D. A. Snow, D. Della Porta, B. Klandermans, and D. McAdam (Eds.), *The Wiley-Blackwell Encyclopedia of Social and Political Movements*. Malden, UK: Wiley.

Staggenborg, S. (2015). *Social Movements* (2nd ed.). New York: Oxford University Press.

Staggenborg, S. (2020). *Grassroots Environmentalism*. Cambridge: Cambridge University Press.

Staggenborg, S., and Meyer, D. A. (2022). "Understanding Countermovements." In D. Tindall, M. C. J. Stoddart, and R. E. Dunlap (Eds.), *Handbook of Anti- Environmentalism* (pp. 23-43). Cheltenham and Camberley, UK:Elgar.

Staggenborg, S., and Taylor, V. (2005). "Whatever Happened to the Women's Movement?" *Mobilization: An International Quarterly*, 10(1), 37–52.

Szasz, A. (2007). *Shopping Our Way to Safety: How We Changed from Protecting the Environment to Protecting Ourselves*. Minnesota, MN: University of Minnesota Press.

Tarrow, S. (1989). *Democracy and Disorder*. Oxford: Oxford University Press.

Taylor, V. (1989). "Social Movement Continuity: The Women's Movement in Abeyance." *American Sociological Review*, 54(5), 761–775.

Tilly, C. (1978). *From Mobilization to Revolution*. Reading, MA: Addison-Wesley.

Tilly, C. (2004). *Social Movements, 1768–2004*. London: Paradigm.

Tomaskovic-Devey, D., and Avent-Holt, D. (2019). *Relational Inequalities: An Organizational Approach*. New York: Oxford University Press.

Van Dyke, N., and Soule, S. A. (2002). "Structural Social Change and the Mobilizing Effect of Threat: Explaining Levels of Patriot and Militia Mobilizing in the United States." *Social Problems*, 49(4), 497–520.

Walker, E. T., and Stepick, L. (2020). "Valuing the Cause: A Theory of Authenticity in Social Movements." *Mobilization: An International Quarterly*, 25(1), 1–25.

Walsh, E., Warland, R., and Smith, D. C. (1997). *Don't Burn it Here: Grassroots Challenges to Trash Incinerators*. University Park, PA: Penn State University Press.

Whittier, N. (2018). "Generational Spillover in the Resistance to Trump." In D. S. Meyer, and S. Tarrow (Eds.), *The Resistance: The Dawn of the Anti-Trump Opposition Movement* (pp. 207–229). New York: Oxford University Press.

Wood, L. J., Suzanne, S., Glenn J. S., and Rachel K.-F. (2017). "Eventful Events: Local Outcomes of G20 Summit Protests in Pittsburgh and Toronto." *Social Movement Studies*, 16(5), 595–560.

Wouters, R . (2019). "The Persuasive Power of Protest: How Protest Wins Public Support." *Social Forces*, 98(1), 403–426.

Wouters, R., and Walgrave, S. (2017). "Demonstrating Power: How Protest Persuades Political Representatives." *American Sociological Review*, 82(2), 361–383.

Acknowledgements

I would like to thank Suzanne Staggenborg and David S. Meyer for their guidance, and the reviewers for their helpful feedback. I would also like to thank Andy Holmes for his help, and Gregory Lograno for helping to produce the video abstract.

Cambridge Elements ≡

Contentious Politics

David S. Meyer
University of California, Irvine

David S. Meyer is Professor of Sociology and Political Science at the University of California, Irvine. He has written extensively on social movements and public policy, mostly in the United States, and is a winner of the John D. McCarthy Award for Lifetime Achievement in the Scholarship of Social Movements and Collective Behavior.

Suzanne Staggenborg
University of Pittsburgh

Suzanne Staggenborg is Professor of Sociology at the University of Pittsburgh. She has studied organizational and political dynamics in a variety of social movements, including the women's movement and the environmental movement, and is a winner of the John D. McCarthy Award for Lifetime Achievement in the Scholarship of Social Movements and Collective Behavior.

About the Series

Cambridge Elements series in Contentious Politics provides an important opportunity to bridge research and communication about the politics of protest across disciplines and between the academy and a broader public. Our focus is on political engagement, disruption, and collective action that extends beyond the boundaries of conventional institutional politics. Social movements, revolutionary campaigns, organized reform efforts, and more or less spontaneous uprisings are the important and interesting developments that animate contemporary politics; we welcome studies and analyses that promote better understanding and dialogue.

Cambridge Elements ⁼

Contentious Politics

Elements in the Series

A full series listing is available at: www.cambridge.org/ECTP